Just A Dog

And the Musings of His Pet

Copyright 2010 by Randy Cribbs

This work relates the shared life adventure of Murphy's Military Maneuver aka "Murphy", an AKC German Shorthaired Pointer and his pet, author Randy Cribbs. Any resemblance to any other actual persons, living or dead, is purely coincidental.
All rights reserved. No part of this book may be reproduced, stored in a retrieval system or transmitted in any form, electronic, mechanical, or by other means, without written permission of the author.

Library of Congress Control Number: 2010900313
ISBN: 9780972579698

Published by OCRS, Inc.
Printed in the United States of America
To obtain books go to www.bn.com;
www.amazon.com ; www.somestillserve.com
or write OCRS, Inc.
P.O. Box 551527
Jacksonville, Florida 32255-1627

Also by Randy Cribbs:

Ghosts : Another Summer in the Old Town

One Summer in the Old Town

Ancient City Treasures

The Vessel: An Ancient City Mystery

Tales from the Oldest City

Were You There? Vietnam Notes

Illumination Rounds [coauthor]

Just A Dog
And The Musings Of His Pet

By
Randy Cribbs

For
My children, grandchildren,
And,

For Murphy

Things are seldom as they appear

As I turned down the long, dark driveway and guided the car toward the carport at the other end, the little red sports car parked there was visible in the dim mercury vapor yard light. I had forgotten to throw the cover over it, but at least the top was up. I babied it far too much.

Something moved. I stopped the car. Movement again, from inside the sportster. I turned the car wheel slightly right so the headlights would hit the convertible and started forward again. The lights reflected off two bright eyes in the rear window of the car.

Wait a minute! There was no rear window. The plastic zip down window was down. But not zipped down. I could now see that the eyes belonged to Murphy, and Murphy was laying on the window inside the car, with convertible top fabric hanging down around his head.

I saw red. Well, the sportster was red, but I saw a darker shade of red. My toy! My indulgence! My mid-life crisis solution! And my dog, laying calmly on the torn window he had obviously jumped through for reasons known only to him.

I awoke with a start and shook my head. A dream. Well, more than a dream. I had been dreaming, but the incident had in fact happened about eight or nine years ago. I was so angry that day, but like most of the stunts Murphy pulled, I got over it. How could I not? It was, after all the Murphy Dog.
We all probably expend too much energy getting mad about stupid things—unimportant things; like predictable behavior. After all, if you know someone or in this case something, is going to behave a certain way, not always to your liking, you ought to just sigh and accept, especially if there's nothing to be done about it. Changing behavior also takes a lot of energy, especially with a beast long out of puppy training.

I couldn't believe I dreamed about that incident after all these years. Another dream about the old fool. Two nights running.

I knew sleep would be hard to find again so I slipped quietly out of bed and felt my way through the bedroom door.

In the early morning darkness of the family room I glanced out the window and noted the river, shimmering under a partial moon, was still there. Reassuring.

I turned toward the couch and listened for the soft snoring of Murphy.

But there was only silence.

My next step in this morning ritual would be to gently touch the dog on his head so he would be warned that the coffee beans were about to be ground. This allowed the 15-year-old beast to gather his senses before the loud noise started. A small thing, but I think he appreciated it.

But Murphy was not there for me to touch.

On this morning, and forever, I would not feel his warm, soft face, or hear the low, contented sigh as he acknowledged my presence.

I knew he wouldn't be there, but the tears came anyway. I wanted him to be there, hoped he would be there, but knew he would not.

Three mornings now I have done this and each morning, against all logic, I listen, feel the empty couch, start coffee, check Murphy's water dish, but it doesn't need filling.

Murphy is gone, but I can't move the dish. I should, but the impossible idea that it may be low on water one morning, signifying his return keeps me from doing so. It's a foolish fantasy; if there's a dish, there is obviously a dog. An old adage I frequently use in jest comes to mind; "things are seldom as they appear." Ironic.

He was old. Fifteen. I knew somewhere deep in my mind that he wouldn't live forever, but I ignored that fact. It felt better buried in my subconscious.

Right flank dog

I have always had dogs. Sixteen over the years. Some were a pain, some a joy. Some lived long lives, and I loved all of them in some fashion, totally bonded with a few. Tiffer for example. She lived a long life; fourteen years. Short hair lab. A blonde beauty. I was so close to that dog. She was five when we got Murphy. Neither Tiffer nor I wanted the six week old beast. Nothing but legs and ears and huge feet. A true German short hair, not the watered down version. He eventually filled out at 95 pounds.

I didn't want him but he showed up with papers and smiles—a gift! His full name, proclaimed on the registration papers being displayed by the bearer of this beast was 'Murphy's Military Maneuvers'. The logic behind the name was explained; I was a soldier and living on a military base on a historic cul de sac called Murphy's Circle. Hence the name. I had to confess it was very original.

Murphy's Military Maneuvers

I had Tiffer. The blonde beauty. My running bud. Why on earth would I want this strange looking beast? Nevertheless, he was here, and my name was on the papers, so I guess I was stuck.

Tiffer trained the beast and did a great job; no easy feat. Though Murphy grew to dwarf her and was much stronger, he bowed to her role as queen dog and later as she aged, he cared for her. As I reflect back, I realize that it was his attitude and behavior toward Tiff that caused me to acknowledge there was more to this big, playful beast than I thought. He mourned for weeks when Tiff died, searching for her around the yard, whimpering. We consoled each other. It was Tiffer's passing that caused the deep bond to develop between Murphy and me. Without either of us realizing it, he slid into her role and became, among other things, my running companion, traveling companion and lounging bud.

Murphy, more so than Tiffer, was a toucher. He never licked, and I liked that, but he always wanted to be touching. The fur on his face and ears was so soft, you could not keep from stroking it. And the ham loved it. The sounds my touch would evoke brought me a sense of calm, a joy that is difficult for some to understand.

Murphy had a PhD in touching. His touch was like a magic wand. It soothed, reassured, gave comfort.

Most dogs are toucher's, though many humans don't touch enough. Dogs know the secret, as do medical professionals who use pets to visit the infirmed and soothe the emotionally wrought. Murphy shared the secret with me freely and often. He was my feel good magic wand for which I awarded him the PhD diploma—doctor Murphy, specialist in the art and science of touching.

Murphy turned out to be a right flank dog. Military term. As a soldier, you always wanted the guys you knew you could count on, those you really trusted, on your right. I've always discreetly categorized friends as right flank guys or 'others'. A good friend can be an other, just not right flank, not the guy you instinctively knew would cover your ass, no matter what. Like my older brother—my big brother. Raymond had a major hand in raising me—no easy task—and for his efforts, received more than one black eye in defense of the sometimes over zealous behavior that defined my youth. He did it without even thinking and still would. Right flank guys. Murphy was a right flank dog.

He didn't ask many questions; he rooted

And, he was a snuggler.

Though pretty much a backyard dog, I began letting Murphy into the house early on. He zeroed in on the couch; my couch. Have you ever shared a couch with a 95-pound beast who felt that he couldn't get close enough to you? The yard dog became a house dog, or more correct, a couch dog.

Thinking I could reclaim my beloved couch, I surprised Murphy with a wonderful orthopedic dog bed. Four feet square and a foot thick. More square footage than my couch; more comfortable than my own bed. He loved it.

He would step onto the bed, make three circles— three— not two or four; three. Then he would lay down; no, he would collapse. He adored it. At least until I stretched out on the couch.

It was a game. I stretched out and he would peer at me with studious eyes, looking for a sign, interpreted by Murphy as any movement on my part. When the signal came, and apparently only Murphy knew the signal, he would stand up, stretch, walk to the couch and stand with his nose three inches from my face. If I looked at him, that apparently was the permission granted sign because up he would come. Not beside me or over me—on me. Ninety five pounds! Adjustments had to be made.

Sometimes, not often, I would surrender the couch and move to an easy chair, at which time Murphy would raise his head, look at me, slide off the couch and return to his bed. If I were feeling particularly mischievous, I would return to the couch. Of course you know what he would do then.

There was a wonderful side benefit to sharing the couch with Murphy other than his 'rooting' to get as close as possible. That was nice, but I also found the real benefit was more intangible.

Before, when I would recline on the couch at days end, I would inevitably think about the day's events, and if it had not been very productive, I would experience some degree of guilt or remorse. That was really stupid! Your day is what it is. There is no requirement to 'set the world on fire' in order to have a good day. Accomplishing nothing sometimes has benefits. Somehow, with that soft head rooting me, accompanied by a myriad of strange sounds, it seemed I could better reconcile the days accomplishments, even if there were none. Living the day somehow became more important than productive results, or perhaps non-productive days became okay. Murphy verified this with his total acceptance of my presence, with or without the days successes or failures; he didn't care. He cared only that I was there. I never had to rehash the day—he didn't ask many questions; he rooted. It worked well.

Larry, Curley, and Moe

Murphy was one year old when we moved back to Florida, to the majestic St Johns River, and he proved to be quite a river dog and a dedicated fisherman, or fisher dog.

I must confess that fishing has never really been a serious affair to me. It provided a setting in which I could reflect, contemplate, or more often, just let my head empty, to practice not subjecting life to scrutiny but rather, live it.

Don't get me wrong, I love to fish. A major part of our two sons' upbringing was fishing. There were many quality hours spent in a boat or on a creek bank, talking, being together. They learned things about the complicated world they were stumbling into. About themselves. It's tough to lose a really big fish or leave the fishing hole while fish are still biting. Those situations to a young lad are as disappointing as real life situations and likewise, have to be dealt with. We all learned things. Fishing is not always about catching fish.

This, however was not a philosophy shared by Murphy.

One of the wonderful things about living on water is a dock that goes over that water. Dock fishing is the essence of relaxation. Thinking. Socializing. Doing nothing. Murphy could not grasp this concept. When it came to fishing, Murphy wanted action, and would ensure that all those on the dock stayed alert for the inevitable tug on the line and the bending of a rod.

After lines were cast into the river, slack tightened, and rods carefully positioned in holders, Murphy took over. While others would kick back in chairs, cool drink in hand, and seek serious relaxation, Murphy would stand poised, centered on the array of poles like a statute, watching the lines for the jerk that signaled a bite. When the jerk came, Murphy would urge the fisherman on with what some friends have called 'the twill'.

The twill was a unique Murphy dog noise made with his tongue; I think. His tense body would tremble as the line was reeled in, the twill would begin softly and grow louder as the end of the line and, hopefully, a fish neared the dock. It was spooky how concentrated he was on the job at hand. I saw that dedicated attitude in my sons years ago when they played video games. They were in the game. They left the rest of the universe. Talking, movement, even yelling could not distract them from that animated screen. If, on the rare occasion they would acknowledge your directions or question with a short, "okay", or "yes", it didn't mean anything, as evidenced by subsequent failure to comply or even remember. Dedicated to the job, like Murphy.

Now the fun part. If there was a fish on the line, it was Murphy's job, as he saw it, to ensure the fish made it safely to the dock floor. He did this by trying to catch the fish in his mouth as it was pulled from the water. Do you begin to see the picture? We have a fisherman working his catch up to grab the flapping body while Murphy assisted by trying to grab the fish, hook and all, in his mouth. It was a spectacle to behold. It was particularly amusing to watch those not familiar with Murphy's antics. Some would get agitated and try to move him aside with a foot or leg since both their hands were busy with the catch.

Beers would be knocked over, folding chairs folded, caps flew off heads. What a show it must have been to those watching from adjacent docks! It surely resembled something out of a Larry, Curley, and Moe scene.

Most would be concerned that Murphy would grab the fish and get hooked. Then there were those who would simply lose control from laughter. My brother did that one time. He was laughing so hard, tears ran down his face, the fish bounced up and down on the end of the line from his convulsions...that is until the fish fell off, causing the hook to slingshot up and hook Raymond's earlobe. I jumped from my chair, knocking it over, Murphy was trying to grab the fish from the deck, Raymond was holding his ear, still laughing. Larry, Curley, and Moe, or in this case, Murphy, Raymond, and Randy—same thing.

Rule one—don't sweat the small stuff
Rule two—everything is small stuff

It's interesting how people react to life's little challenges, the ups and downs. Their actions can tell you things. Some go into a tizzy, even panic over the most simple things. I remind friends, and myself on such occasions of a philosophy rule I heard many years ago. It's a two part rule: part one, don't sweat the small stuff; part two, everything is small stuff. I never had to teach the Murphy dog that rule because he was obviously born knowing it. I wish there was an annual shot for us, like a flu shot, except this new shot would serve to remind us of the rule until the next shot was due. Probably save a lot of heated discussions.

Whatever behavior category the fishermen experiencing Murphy's antics fell into-humor, anger, panic-had zero impact on Murphy. His job was to secure the fish. Like a good soldier, that was his mission, and he did whatever it took to accomplish that mission. If only we were all that focused!

You can't move 95 pounds with a leg. Yelling only made him work harder at his job. I think he probably regarded yelling as we would cheering, so he responded with gusto. Laughter insulted him because landing a fish is serious business.

There were times Murphy would manage to grab the fish in his mouth. He never got hooked, and more amazing to me was the gentle way he would hold the wiggling fish. No biting and obviously no intent to eat it. The down side was that he wouldn't give the fish back right away. We learned that if you were patient, he would drop the fish after a while, or you could trick him. It was discovered, quite by accident, that if you turned your attention from Murphy and his catch and grabbed one of the outcast rods as if a lunker was hooked, the Murphy dog would immediately release his victim and turn his attention to the new challenge—helping land the next fish. He understood priorities.

Don't sweat the small stuff...everything is small stuff. I wish I had originated that rule, but I didn't. Murphy may have, because he used it so well, apparently without conscious thought. Everything to him was small stuff. I observed him frequently, standing with a confused look on his face, when suddenly, he would lay down. Within seconds, he was fast asleep. I can only surmise that he forgot what he was doing, so he simply took a nap. The essence of the rule.

Don't sweat the small stuff...a great stress reducer. Murphy knew how to avoid stress. He didn't worry over things that he couldn't figure out or that were beyond his comprehension, and that included quite a lot. If something did bother him and he couldn't eat it or play with it, he'd just lift his leg, mark it, and walk off. There you have it; everything is small stuff.

...but then, he was the master

Murphy responded to reality more than words. That's the way dogs are. There are many people who can spew forth an abundance of words which don't seem to be grounded in reality; and not just politicians. They do it best, but there are many others who also do it well. It doesn't really seem honest when you do that. There should be a rule; words need to be connected to reality! Murphy was connected to reality. He couldn't talk—well, maybe sometimes—so his actions were driven by the now and the end result. Because of that simple trait, you always knew what Murphy meant and where he stood on things. There was no veil thrown over meaningless words to hide or camouflage his intent or true feelings. We, on the other hand, might say or think, "I should cut the grass." We don't want to cut the grass! That's what we should say because that's what our words or thoughts are saying. That's what Murphy would do. His actions replaced words and took out all the guesswork. Your words are you; your behavior is you. Another novel concept we could all do well to practice.

The gentle way Murphy held a fish was reflective of his nature. Anyone could hand him a treat, under any circumstances, and he would take it from their hand so softly they could hardly feel it. People were always amazed at how gentle the huge beast was. It was just his nature. I believe all dogs are naturally self-centered. It's a survival instinct. But they can also be sensitive. I know Murphy was self-centered. He was a dog. But there were so many times, maybe most of the time, when he just seemed to do things or not do things to please me. Even now, I'm not sure which one of us was more concerned for the other's welfare. I believe Murphy knew he wasn't just my dog; he was my partner.

He enjoyed the moment, whatever it was, which in turn caused me to enjoy the moment. I needed that because I confess there were too many times in my life that I didn't do that—just be in the moment.

What is that drive we have to go after some 'thing', often not even defined, that we want to do or be or have or whatever, instead of simply being in the moment, even with just ourselves? I started doing that more and found that I really enjoyed myself. Same thing with our fascination about things yet to happen. Murphy never thought about the future. In past times, I would think about the future and experience anxiety. A fear that goals would not be achieved, or things would not work out as planned. Murphy did get anxious, but only if it involved food or a chase. Now, more and more, I regard the future as an impending adventure, not an event that should cause anxiety. I have never gotten as good as the Murphy dog was with this process but then he was the master.

...his head would emerge with...nothing

Murphy was sometimes very hard-headed, particularly if he was in the river hunting and I wanted him out. Oh, didn't I mention that? The Murphy dog was a great hunter, and his favorite hunting ground was in the river. He owned it. He was the king of that domain, master of all that resided there.

The water level at the near end of my dock was seldom deeper than Murphy's shoulder. Sometimes, depending on the tide, only to his knees. Because of this, I got the bright idea to build a ramp, complete with gate, so the dogs could amble down to cool off in the hot Florida summer. There was a minor problem.

In water that shallow you can see fish.

Murphy had no interest in cooling off. Murphy was interested—no, more like obsessed—in hunting fish. The great hunter would stalk, moving carefully through the water, stopping, watching, muscles quivering. Then, his nub of a tail would go up and out as he thrust his head under the water, way under, to grab his prey; small perch or redbreast or whatever was moving. Seconds later his head would emerge with—nothing. Well, nothing other than ribbon grass hanging from his nose and ears. In all the years, the countless hours he spent at this endeavor, he never caught a fish, or anything else. How can a dog catch a swimming fish? But, he never tired of trying, and I never tired of watching him try. I don't think he cared whether or not he caught anything. He loved it. Some people worried about a gator getting him. I worried about that as well, but risk is inherent in some endeavors, and it was such a pleasure for him. There was nothing I could do. He loved it so I loved it, because I understood.

The Murphy dog could have been prowling the yard, chasing lizards or frogs. That's hunting, but considerably more safe. No gators, no moccasins, no crabs. The crabs did get him a few times. But the water hunting was so much more exciting. The element of risk, maybe. I understood because I must confess I was on occasion the same way. Motorcycles, jumping out of perfectly good airplanes, going in harm's way, sometimes of my own accord. Those activities and others have some elements in common: challenge, different, not easy, not the norm. Foolish risks are stupid, but some risks remind us that we are actually alive.

During his water activities, I often wondered what I would do if a gator came after him. Murphy would not have retreated; he was the king. But would I have gone in?
Yes. I would have. That isn't just bravado, or a macho statement after the fact, it's what I'd do. To me, it would have been no different than my view of situations in Vietnam, or risky training, or chasing bad guys. If your bud needs help, you help. Murphy was my bud. I would have gone in without even thinking about it. I am happy to report however, that it never became a requirement.

The kid in me reincarnated...

While watching the great hunter gave me hours of enjoyment, getting him out of the water...well, not so much. He would not leave the water.

Murphy was obsessed with the hunt. So much so that when he needed to pee (for some unknown reason, he would not do that in the water) he would stalk, glance at the walkway, the route to relief, stalk again, glance at the walkway again, whine, and resume the stalk. Finally, when the urge overwhelmed his hunting passion, he would charge up the ramp to the yard and lift the old leg. During the relief process, his eyes would be fixed on me, keeper of the gate. They pleaded, those eyes, as if saying, 'please don't shut the gate, I'll be right back'.
I didn't.

Even when I needed him out because of time constraints. I just never had the heart to close that gate; to deprive him of his passion. I could relate. As a kid, there was a great, open field across the street from our house. It's where we played pickup ball; baseball, football, all kind of ball. We were passionate. Routinely, before the games were through, the loud voices of several mom's would be yelling out from the houses, 'Dinner, come in.' We ignored the yells. The game was not finished. When agitated moms or worse, dads, would leave houses and start across the street, we responded. There were lessons learned here-consideration for others, all good things must end, self-discipline, and of course, the consequences of perceived bad behavior. In subsequent years, I would think how cool it would be to be able to pursue a passion until you were done; until you made the choice to stop, a choice not forced by others. A choice that would just happen, naturally. How cool would that be?

I couldn't close that gate. I was Murphy, playing, having fun, being a kid, with nothing in my head but the game at hand. But the Murphy dog did not reciprocate.

The one thing Murphy would ignore was my request for him to leave the water; to end the hunt. Wouldn't happen. He would not end the hunt until the hunt was over, defined by him. Not for food, not for my lowered, scolding voice or my exasperated yells—not for anything. But I understood. It was sometimes painful, but I understood. Everyone has a passion; I mean, a true passion, and that was Murphy's.

I could have figured some devious plan to get him out of the water, but there was nothing really all that important to deprive the Murphy dog of his passion. What's a few cold meals, or missed appointments, or, yes, canceled events! Stupid, I know but he would have done the same for me. It was just part of his unique behavior, and because I grew to accept that, it wasn't necessarily bad, or inappropriate.

We all know people with certain behavior traits we don't particularly like or agree with, but that doesn't mandate that we should not accept them. It does not require compromise or effort to accept a person who acts or behaves as we would like, but work is required if we aren't "on the same sheet of music." So what!

You cannot put conditions on personality or passion-driven behavior. If you can't change it, or more appropriately, if there is really no good reason to change it other than our own disapproval, accept it. Be the way you are. The free pursuit of passion, which other than the occasional aggravation, is really no big deal. How could I do less for the Murphy dog; for the kid in me reincarnated?

The phenomenon, the rudder, the...nub

By the way, the nub tail I mentioned was six and one-quarter inches long. A friend and I measured it one time. I wanted to know what made it tick. It was the Murphy dog barometer. From that tail, I learned things about Murphy. It was his mood indicator, his alert meter, his "don't bother me" signal, his great hunter game pointer, his rudder. It required kneading, like the muscles of an athlete. Right at the base where it joined his ample butt. I was his masseur, and I could evoke noises not of this world probing that nub. It was spooky.

When he strolled leisurely down the driveway or out the three hundred foot long pier leading to the boat lift, the tail would always be jutting up and out at a ninety degree angle. My friend suggested it may act as a stabilizer, similar to those on an airplane or fast car.

He rationalized this theory by pointing out that Murphy didn't walk; he swaggered. Remember the John Wayne swagger? Same thing. That swagger oozed cool and calm, no hurry, in control. Like Murphy. Except for the nub. While he swaggered, the tail seemed to remain in a constant position. Is that possible?

Murphy did lose a little swagger one time, though only briefly. He was always a healthy dog, boring for the vet as far as health challenges were concerned. We would show up for the annual check: worm check, blood check, a shot then we were out of there, or at least we would've been if it weren't for Murphy hamming it for the vet staff, who adored him.

But then things changed when during an annual vet visit, the vet announced that Murphy should be 'fixed'. She explained that as old as he was, the potential for certain problems become more probable, and fixing him would solve that.

Fixed. When she said the word, I was speechless. So was Murphy. He jerked his head up when she uttered the word. I think he understood, and he didn't appear crazy about the idea.

A strange choice of word for that procedure. Fixed. More like break. I suspect any male reading this just winced. I did. It causes undesirable images to flash through one's mind. I also worried that he might not forgive me. Would you? Nevertheless, convinced, I consented. It went well and he healed almost overnight, but the swagger suffered for a few days. Before, his 'pendulum' set acted as a counter-balance which enhanced the swagger. With the balance weights gone, he had to adjust. He actually stumbled a couple of times. Then, he would stop and look back as if confused. I couldn't think of anything to say.

Fortunately, this dilemma lasted only a short while, and before long the old Murphy swagger was back. Different, but back. Just goes to show that we can all adjust to life's changes, even in the most dire circumstances. I am also happy to report that the tail, the infamous nub, did not suffer. Its' signals remained constant.

It was amazing what that tail could reveal, but you had to know how to read it, not unlike maritime flag signals which are nothing more than a bunch of flapping flags, unless you can read them. I became quite adept at reading the nub signals. Some signals did not require interpretation—the thunder signal, for example.

Murphy was afraid of thunder. No, not afraid. Terrified. It was the only thing this big, strong beast truly feared. He would stand his ground against any creature, but when it thundered, he would tremble and cower, whimpering like a pup, his nub tail tucked down so far you couldn't see it. It was a pathetic picture. I felt bad for him, but there was nothing I could do, other than let him press against me.

Most living things have been afraid in certain situations, but I think in most cases, that's different than true fear, like Murphy must have felt. Some people can relate to that—to true fear. I sympathized with the Murphy dog because I experienced fear a couple of times. In Vietnam I felt fear. It felt bad and, worse, it never really goes away. Murphy was like that. If a car backfired, he would immediately alert and seek me out until he was sure the sound was not thunder. Then he was okay. That type of fear was always with him. It was the single event that caused him to be totally out of sorts. Humans can think through their fear logically. Dissect it. Cause-effect-resolution. Dogs can't do that. They don't understand. Imagine how terrible that must be; to fear something you don't understand and therefore can't control.

The nub signal I particularly treasured was the subtle, but rapid wiggle when I walked in or spoke. It was Murphy's acknowledgement that I was present, or speaking, or moving. I was with him, and he was glad. So was I.

Reverification

Murphy practiced a life of reverification. Most dogs do this, and all male dogs do it. Not verification, but reverification; that's when you verify over and over and over and...so on. Murphy would do this in many ways, such as sniffing the same bushes every time he went outside, as if to verify they were still there. Sometimes they would not be; a bush would be gone because I had cut it away (I have a thing with bushes that slow down the mowing process). He didn't like it, as evidenced by the disapproving look I would get. Nevertheless, he would promptly mark the spot to reverify that the spot, if not the bush, was still his. He would watch me during the marking process, then scratch grass and dirt and move on his merry way. I think that may have been both a sign of disapproval and a reminder that he still claimed that area, in spite of its vacancy.

Likewise, many times when we would be hanging out, he would get up for no apparent reason, walk up to me and touch his nose to my leg and do a quick sniff. I deducted that he was reverifying my presence, or that it was in fact me.

Then of course, there was THE verification—the lick; you know, THE lick. Murphy conducted this operation several thousand times a day and always methodically, with purpose. This was obviously a major, necessary reverification. It was one of his more serious rules; one that required he do it a given number of times each day. Only Murphy knew the number, but I could always tell when he was behind in the count, because he accelerated the repetitions, as if trying to catch up on the count. Now, this is a male dog rule, not just a Murphy rule, although Murphy could have certified as a Zen Master because he didn't just lick aimlessly—it was procedural, a process, refined over the years, done without thought.

My friends and I marveled at the process. We made comments, to which Murphy would briefly acknowledge with a condescending look, then continue his endeavor, oblivious to his audience and any remarks made regarding the practice of this very serious rule. His purpose was single-minded, focused. No one ever figured out the exact purpose, though as you might imagine, the voiced opinions ran a wide range—none of which seemed to hinder Murphy in his endeavor.

Humans seek and practice reverification, particularly in matters of our worth—how people perceive us. That's good, because by doing so, we acknowledge we also care about others—their view is important, particularly regarding us personally. I'm not sure whether or not Murphy had that concept in mind with the licking process, but surely he did when he would touch his nose to me to verify my presence, or to get my attention.

He would charge around the yard making strange noises, grabbing sticks and tossing them about. No doubt his antics frightened every living creature in proximity, certainly frogs and lizards because they could be seen darting for cover to avoid the rampaging beast. He always finished this show by running up to me for the head scratch and words of praise; both of which he knew he would get. A reverification that I approved; I accepted his behavior, no matter how strange. After the scratch, he would drop to the ground and conduct licking reverification while he rested and regrouped.

After the beast was neutered late in his life, he still performed the licking ritual, though with slightly less exuberance. It seemed that during the process to reverify, he noted something missing. He would be performing his act, then cease operations and give me a quizzical look. Each time he did this, I would explain the situation, after which he would resume the process, throwing me an occasional dirty look. I suspected he was looking for a sign that the process would bring his friends back, but I couldn't give him one.

Playing with frogs...a genetic trait

Murphy amused himself in many ways. He did this without effort, probably without thinking; it was natural. We should be so lucky! I suspect we could probably learn to do it with practice, though certainly not as well as Murphy or most other dogs. For us, unlike dogs, there would be some risks. After all, if we learned to amuse ourselves too much, 'people would talk'. More dangerous, we might like it; amusing ourselves for no reason other than to amuse ourselves. When I was a kid, I sometimes amused myself with frogs. Funny little creatures, frogs. People paid no attention then, but if I did it now...well, not such a good idea, although I would have a good excuse—it's genetic.

I say that because when my youngest son was nine or ten, he had a fascination with frogs. He formed a club with several of his friends, the single purpose of which was to catch frogs, put them in carefully constructed boxes attached to bicycles, and roar around the neighborhood with Mom's towels (you must have a cape) trailing behind in the breeze. The 'Toadbuster's'. They had a sign and probably even bylaws regarding the size and hopping capability of each toad. The toads were well cared for, each rotated and released every couple of days to retain vigor and, I suppose, life. To this day, my son's nickname to those of us who recall his reign as President of The Toadbusters is of course, Toad. Genetic. Also transferable by close association to dogs, evidenced by Murphy's fondness for frogs.

They amused him; another trait he and I had in common. I enjoy watching frogs and lizards. A lizard seems to move with purpose; a frog, not so much. Sometimes I pick them up and stare into their eyes. They stare back. Lizards seem more anxious when I do this, but frogs seem very nonchalant about the interruption. I am always gentle with them and do not cause injury. I even brake for frogs and lizards when I'm mowing and remain stopped until I'm sure they're clear. That would make a great bumper sticker: 'I brake for frogs'. The beast was careful as well. Murphy would spot a frog, approach it, and lay straight down on his chest and stomach, paws out and on either side of the startled creature. When the frog hopped, Murphy's tail would go up and move at 22,000 r.p.m.'s, then, he would slide forward on his belly to the frog and wait for the next hop.

When it came, he repeated the maneuver. If the frog hopped to close to a bush or some other cover, Murphy would lay a big paw on it, then lift it, as if to encourage the toad to change direction. Occasionally, that strategy worked; most of the time it didn't. The frog would disappear and Murphy would move to the next adventure, or, if it was a pleasant day, he would simply roll over in place and take a snooze. Amusing yourself is easy when everything amuses you. Like chasing squirrel's. He enjoyed that as much as the frog game, though he was never much good at it, at least the catching part.

    He caught several other unsuspecting creatures—he was, after all, a hunter—but, he never caught a squirrel.

Squirrel games...and perspective

There are few guarantees in life. That's good, because it keeps things interesting. There are, however, some things on which one can depend. For instance, when Murphy and I would go onto the dock, he would walk straight to his swim ramp gate, thinking it was fish hunt time. Guaranteed.

Likewise, it became clear early on that he would never catch a squirrel. Guaranteed.

Another guarantee is that squirrels, who have a fondness for playing on the shoulder of roads, will not go all the way across a road in one run when a car is bearing down on them. They go halfway, hop straight up, then go back the way they came—into the path of the car. What's up with that?

There does not seem to be a reasonable explanation for this behavior, but there is a guarantee that you can plan for it. If Murphy had figured out this predictable behavior, he could have left the squirrel hunting preserve (our yard) and increased his chance of success in catching one. He either never figured that out, or he preferred his private preserve.

Our yard is full of squirrels and, not unlike his fish hunting, he never grew tired of stalking the little animals. If his squirrel hunting had been a game of horseshoes, he would have a ton of points for coming close, but no ringers. I enjoyed watching Murphy, and the squirrels, as he stalked them over every square inch of the yard. It is important to note that he didn't just chase squirrels; oh no. It was a stealthy, methodical, patient stalk.

He would move one paw forward and gently touch the ground, as if feeling for dry twigs which, if broken under his foot, would alert the prey. It was amazing to watch his tensed, crouched body move ever so slow, his eyes focused on the foraging squirrel, the nub quivering. If the squirrel turned his back to Murphy, the hunter would increase his speed slightly and then stop to ensure he had not been detected. This cat and mouse action would go on for several minutes until the squirrel realized he was not alone and bolt for the nearest tree. That's when Murphy would charge forward, to no avail.

He never went after the squirrel until it was making a beeline to safety. On many occasions, even I could see that had he charged at the right moment, when he was close and the squirrel was in the open, he might have caught the creature. But he never did.

I could not figure out why he never struck when the opportunity presented itself. I've done that before. Inaction when I should have taken action. Waiting, instead of "striking when the iron was hot." Maybe it was just a game with Murphy. He did enjoy his games. Maybe it never occurred to him to take his play to a more serious level. It just didn't seem to matter. When I fail to take advantage of an opportunity, it gnaws at me. I beat myself up, make excuses for my oversight.

Most of us are taught from an early age to look for and seize opportunities. Most of the time, a good rule, but not always. Simply because an opportunity presents itself doesn't always mean it's best to take it. With Murphy, the game was the stalk; not catching the prey. That worked for him. That was the game. Period. I think I might try that the next time I miss an opportunity. I'll try harder to appreciate the adrenalin rush, the logical thought leading to the 'should I or should I not decision', and if in doing that, the opportunity passes me by,

I'll say, "What a cool experience that was." The opportunity may be gone, but I won't be chastising myself. Just chalk it up and wait for the next game—like the Murphy dog, except I don't think I'll be as good at it.

The Murphy persona

Murphy, like most dogs, acted in character in almost all situations. He was Murphy and his behavior was Murphy. This is a trait I studied because I required work and practice in some situations. Specifically, formal settings. In that environment, I tended to be on guard, too concerned with what people thought because in those situations, there are accompanying expectations. Social gatherings are supposed to be fun, a social event, but instead, I sometimes had a tendency to be alert in order to respond or act in the "appropriate manner."

I learned from the Murphy dog that while you shouldn't be a buffoon, you can be yourself and have a more enjoyable time. It required conscious thought initially, but then, it became natural—because it was natural. It was me. While it would not have been prudent to be as free and natural as Murphy—I wouldn't chew fleas, or other things, in the middle of a conversation—I did find these gatherings far more enjoyable. The added benefit was new acquaintances actually knew Randy by the time the event was over and not some other person. Still though, I must confess it would have been more fun to chew fleas in some of the more boring social settings. One has to compromise in most things...unless of course, you're the Murphy dog.

I just became aware that every few pages I have been referring to Murphy as the Murphy dog. Somewhere in time over the past several years, Murphy's Military Maneuvers—Murphy—became to some, the Murphy dog.

I don't recall initiating that. In fact, I'm sure I didn't. I have looked deep into the past buried in my head in an attempt to figure when that started, and by whom, but to no avail. I do have a theory.

Murphy dog, as opposed to simply Murphy is both respectful and personal. It suggests a unique persona. Over the years, those who knew Murphy, even if only briefly, loved him. Not just the old 'hey, Murphy dog', accompanied by the obligatory head scratch and then on to what brought them. No. Their hand would linger on that soft head. They would engage him in conversation when in fact, they were supposed to be visiting me.

Murphy had many qualities, as with most dogs, but something else as well. Other things. Things hard to put your finger on. True, he had personality galore, and he didn't inflict himself on you. No jumping on you, no licking, no barking for attention. Yet, he made you want to give him attention. I have watched him weave that magic with people. It gave me some comfort to see that I wasn't the only fool in the house!

All of us really enjoy being with certain people. Now, picture being with that special person and you get to do all the talking, and the other party agrees with everything, even your silence. Their looks and actions approve and reassure. You can do no wrong. Crazy, I know, but that was Murphy's persona. He was a dog, so obviously he didn't study this technique, and surely was not even aware of the effect; it was just the vibes he gave off.

I like to believe, whether it's true or not, that the way Murphy was treated by my family made him family, with most of the rights any family member enjoys. Wherever I was, Murphy was with me; in the house, the man room, the dock, the yard. It could be that because Murphy knew how much he was loved, he didn't need to get all over you to command attention. He was a part of it all, not unlike a child who acts with the knowledge that he is seen, heard, and accepted, as opposed to committing foolish acts to draw attention. One of my friends has a beautiful dog that is confined to a four by six foot cage. He seldom gets to run the big, spacious, fenced yard because 'his urine kills the grass'. He has never been inside the house. In the words of one of my Army buddies, "that just ain't right." A person should not have a pet if they can't, or won't, integrate it into the family and accept the tradeoffs. Ought to be a rule.

Of course, too much attention can turn a perfectly good dog, also not unlike a child, into a ham.

Several years ago, I made the mistake of writing Murphy into my second book and then three subsequent books. Bit parts which helped to set characters or scenes. Then, some idiot got the idea to include Murphy in my 'about the author'; his picture, no less! Not only did that go to his head, it shifted attention from me to him. Can you believe it! I did the work, and a dog got the attention.

Thereafter, friends, business associates, and yes, readers would greet me like this: "Hey, how's it goin'? how's the Murphy dog?" Get the picture?

Yesterday, I went to town for the first time since Murphy's passing. Upon entering a small bookstore, my favorite place nestled in the heart of the Old Town, guess how I was greeted by one of the charming ladies who own that shop? Of course you know.

I could not respond. The store owner's concerned look confirmed what I suspected; there were tears rolling down my face.

I turned and left. No choice. I could not speak. I thought briefly about what two staring customers must have been thinking. Didn't really care, though. It seemed so unimportant, their thoughts.

Funny how we are like that. On one day, or in certain situations, perhaps around certain people, we concern ourselves about how we are viewed. Other times, not so much.

Some hours later I called the owner back to apologize and explain my behavior. I could hear her sobbing. I quickly said that I would call her later and hung up.

So there you have it. This lady had read about Murphy in some of my books, and had listened to me regaling customers about the dog in the picture, but she had never seen him.

See how we are? I plan to ask her later who she grieved for—me or Murphy? It doesn't matter because either way, a connection somewhere along the way had been made. She cared, and when we care about something, or someone, our humanness comes out. I think it's good that we reaffirm from time to time that we have a soul, and life is not just about me. It's dangerous, emotionally, to let a living thing go too deep into your soul. Dangerous, but necessary to reaffirm who we are; what is important, that maybe some of those problems plaguing us are not really that important.

Murphy never seemed to have that many problems and was very clear regarding what he did or did not want to do. For instance, when I would throw the tennis ball for a game of fetch, he would charge out and grab the ball. However, if he was not interested, he would stay in place, watching me to see if there was a better offer. No excuses. No apologies. If he was not inclined to chase a ball, he didn't. I, on the other hand, have made excuses for not wanting to go somewhere or do something. Rather than simply saying, "No thank you, I don't want to," I would offer some lame, fictitious excuse.

I would do well to emulate Murphy in his honesty. Being honest didn't seem to bother him and probably wouldn't bother me if done in a gracious manner, although the Murphy dog never seemed to be concerned with the gracious part.

Politics, religion, and dog philosophy

Murphy was a good dog and a happy dog. Well, good most of the time. He was happy because he had me and we understood each other. He was happy because he found pleasure in such simple things. He didn't pay any attention to politics, he professed no religion that I could determine, and a quest for knowledge was beyond his pay grade. He was happy. Most dogs are. We humans, however, while we can be happy, long for knowledge. We are willing to make great sacrifices, take perilous journeys to attain knowledge; a frustrating endeavor on occasion.

I'm sure Murphy had no concept of God, and while man can never understand the motivations of a Supreme Being, our yearning for understanding may promote in us the essence of the concept- truth and goodness. That has been said by all manner of man, in every way possible throughout history, so there must be something to it.

Murphy understood when it was time to eat, sleep, and play; that was his truth and goodness. I envied his quest. I envied even more that he achieved it daily. The great philosophers all agree, as do I, that the pleasures of earth can never satisfy man; we think too much. When we think too much, we start to fret about what should have been, or what lies ahead and how we can influence what is yet to come. That can complicate or detract from the now. Murphy's outlook—to be, to do—seems less stressful.

There was at least one trait among the intangibles I shared with Murphy; a belief that life is good. It's worthwhile even though there are times it doesn't seem so. We share that with out dogs, though they recover from despair far faster and without obvious lasting mental anguish. I told Murphy that though I envied his lack of the other traits, I particularly envied his ability to better handle the one we share. He yawned. See what I mean. No thinking. No dwelling on short lived negatives. Disappointment vanished when a frog or lizard caught his eye. Presto. Depression gone. Can that be practiced? Should the great philosophers have studied dogs rather than us frail humans? By the way, many of those guys had dogs so maybe there was canine input. Even the great thinker and philosopher Plato once said, "A dog has the soul of a philosopher." Smart fellow, Plato.

Watching Murphy, I often wondered what kind of memory he and his fellow canines have. Short term, long term—none. When I picked up his leash, he became excited and stretched because he knew the leash meant a walk. Obviously some kind of memory there, if association counts as memory. On the other hand, if a person he had not seen for a long period of time appeared, he would display no signs of recognition until he sniffed the visitor. I deduced that there was a link between smell and memory. Seems logical anyway.

Humans seem to have a complicated memory process. Some things we can recall in detail, some only slightly, and some, not at all. Some memories never fade. I have many great memories as well as some not so great, but nothing in my memory bank has ever supplanted the time I spent in combat. Not the gruesome events, but the soldiers I shared that time with. The sense of unity, comradeship. I can recall insignificant scenes and even conversations in remarkable detail even after forty plus years. I have never understood that.

Play was significant to Murphy, and I think he had long term memory of anything associated with play.

When my son and his family visited from out of town, Murphy, upon seeing Mike, would immediately start sniffing around for Mike's dog, Cedar, with whom Murphy enjoyed playing games. If Cedar had not made the trip, I could detect disappointment in Murphy's demeanor. Maybe dogs can pick which events to remember and discard all others. If so, what would you give for that gift? To be able to recall only pleasant events and black out the unpleasant or boring.

Dogs just don't seem to get bored; at least that was true about the Murphy dog. With us, when it comes to having things to do or nothing to do, we either complain that we have too much to do, or on the other side, we're bored because we either have nothing to do or whatever we're doing does not appeal to us.

Murphy never had too much to do because he took one step at a time, one sniff at a time. When that was done, he went to the next item of interest. Likewise, if he had nothing to do, or his interest faltered, he went to sleep—he did nothing. That's right, he did nothing, and he was really good at it.

Watch your dog doing nothing. They do that routinely and most are experts—like the Murphy dog. Now you try it. Do nothing. See what I'm talking about. It isn't easy. Master—pet. Pet—master. You pick.

All things for all situations...
Hunter, runner, bully

Though never trained as a hunting dog, Murphy could point, stalk, creep, and lay low. One of my uncles, a big bird hunter who trained and hunted bird dogs was always amazed at how adept Murphy was at the art and pleaded with me to let him hunt. I couldn't do that! He was a natural hunter, yes. But no one told him. To him it was a game. Stalking lizards, frogs and when feeling particularly mischievous, Tiffer. That really made the Queen nervous. Murphy would look so serious, she would back away. Then without warning, Murphy would shed the hunter persona and charge around the old gal in ever decreasing circles, finally rolling at her feet, large paws touching her, ever so gently, as if to reassure her, and me, that he was only kidding.

It was an acceptable form of bullying. If apparent aggressive behavior has some meaningful goal or objective, it's okay. On the other hand, if it is self serving with no other productive end—not acceptable. Military drill sergeants are experts at productive bullying. Their actions are zeroed in on specific, positive end results, including intimidating a trainee into doing something that ultimately instills confidence. Murphy's goal was not self serving because clearly he was attempting to involve Tiffer in his play and ultimately fell at her feet, renewing her Queen status. Positive bullying from the Murphy dog.

To turn that behavior, that game-like perspective into a serious, formal affair would have been a crime. More important, it would not have been Murphy. A serious hunter could never understand that. Too bad. Their loss, not mine or Murphy's.

For many years, Murphy was my running bud. I did, however, decide a couple of years ago that maybe walking wasn't so bad. I think Murphy agreed. But before that, we would go to a large, primitive, wooded area near here, complete with miles of rough fire trails and run. Together for several miles, then having had enough, I would stop and turn back. Murphy would stop and give me the old "What are you doing?" look. I would wave my arm and say, "Go ahead", and off he would go at full speed, fire trail dirt flying from under feet that barely touched the ground. I think I saw smoke trailing behind him on occasion!

Unfortunately, this became a habit, and I have waited for more than an hour for him to return, exhausted, long tongue dragging the ground, gulping the water I always had with us. He would be absolutely wasted, but happy. He loved it. He lived for it. I feel a similar sense of freedom when I ride my cycle down Highway 13 with the wind in my face and the majestic St. Johns River on my right. I'm enjoying the scenery, I'm free, in control, and though Murphy could not accompany me on those excursions, he would approve because I have fun—a subject he knows much about.

Truth in Murphy ads

Things are seldom as they appear. Did I mention that earlier?

As I sat in the yard chillin' [I frequently do that], Murphy would be doing likewise. The breeze would flow through my hair while my mind uncluttered, floated. It's a process that allows some of the 'stuff' in my head to travel out through my ears into the environment. Murphy cooperated, though nothing went out through his ears because of their size and weight, but his soft snore relaxed me, and I was grateful he was settled in. Everything was in a state of serenity, but things are seldom as they appear.

Without warning, Murphy would jump up, shake, and charge about like an idiot, shattering any possibility of further mind cleansing. Now, what was that all about? Was he feigning sleep while waiting for the right moment to go crazy? Was he dreaming and decided to act out? Was he messing with me? That was the more likely possibility. In any event, because it was a stunt he pulled on occasion, I knew what to expect—no false advertisement, no misleading statements or promises, unlike the car lube place I stopped by the other day to get an oil change.

Their big sign said, "oil change, $18.95 plus tax. They completed the work and handed me the bill; $23.15. The breakdown: $18.95 for parts and labor; $1.20 tax; $3.00 handling fee. I asked what the handling fee was about, to which he replied that it was for processing and everyone paid it. "Then your oil change is really $21.95 plus tax, not $18.95 plus tax as your sign and literature states," I stated. "No, it's $18.95; the three bucks is a separate fee," he responded. I quickly determined that this conversation was going nowhere, so I applied the Murphy law [that's where I think about what Murphy might do in a similar situation]; I yawned and left.

Now, even Murphy could figure out that the oil change was not $18.95; it was $21.95. This situation would be unacceptable under the Truth in Murphy rule and should be under anyone's rule, although like Murphy's antics, we seem to be conditioned to accept an end result not in keeping with promises made. We should all unite and force business back to the days of bartering. All things would be negotiable. Make a reasonable counteroffer and the other guy would take it or leave it. If we all did that, if it became the norm, I suspect a barter fairness doctrine would evolve, and misleading crap would fall away.

This concept was not unfamiliar to Murphy, because I used it with him routinely. For instance, if I were reclining in the chair reading and the beast wanted to play, but I didn't, I would relocate to the couch—so would he. He slept, I read. Bartering.

Be straightforward in what you offer; don't make me work to figure things out, and don't mislead me; or be prepared to barter.

Things are seldom as they appear. A dog I forgive. A misleading advertisement I don't.

But the cat came back...and stayed

There was a cat. Cheddar. Ironically, Cheddar died in his sleep just three months before Murphy. They had an interesting relationship for many years. Have you ever had a neighbor whom you didn't particularly care for, so because there was nothing to be done about it, you just tolerated each other? That was Murphy and Cheddar; at least until they both got pretty old.

Cheddar wandered up to the house a long time ago. I can't even remember how many years, but a lot. Knowing Murphy's opinion of cats, I tried for days to get Cheddar to leave, but the large yellow cat would not go, so I gave up and started feeding him. Besides, Cheddar hung out in the front yard, while Murphy was usually either in the house or the backyard, lounging on the dock. At some point during the day, my habit was to open the gate separating the front and back yards so Murphy could run the entire yard and keep track of the various creatures that come and go in the night.

He did this by smell and what is delicately referred to as marking.

It amazed me how many times he could leave his mark in one outing. What's up with that? I have heard the many explanations, and some do make sense, but I have my own theory, at least in Murphy's case. He wasn't marking his territory, or issuing a challenge, or setting up his defensive perimeter. Those were just Murphy's excuses. He did it because he was having fun! He did it because he could, and because he wanted to. Who needs a reason to do something that's fun?

Oh, how I envied him! The reckless abandon of it all. Doing something because you want to-- because it gives you pleasure. Because you can. Another great concept! Not unlike me saying, "I really want that candy bar. I don't need it, but I want it. It won't hurt anyone, it's me eating it. I want it."

Dogs act intuitively, and they seem to have more fun. When I use my intuitive instincts, I am more focused and feel better. But if I question whether or not I really want to do something, that's confused intuition. That would be like the Murphy dog contemplating chasing a lizard but not moving—ain't gonna happen. Consider the intuition option even when it may seem foolish. Another Murphy lesson; it's okay to be an idiot every now and then. So what!? But back to Cheddar.

For years, Murphy chased Cheddar. I opened the gate, out shot Murphy, looking for the yellow intruder. It became another game. When the cat would see me heading toward the gate to unleash the beast, he would actually move closer, get in his best sprinter's stance, and await the gun—or in this case, the gate latch clang. Then they were off!

It's hard for a dog to catch a cat when the cat knows he's there and has maneuver room, so he never did catch him. But then, thanks in part to the wisdom of getting old, the game changed. Murphy had now become a house dog (embarrassing) complete with sagging muscles, arthritis, and terrible breath. One day I opened the door as usual so Murphy could take a run and he and Cheddar could have their little chase, except this time, Cheddar didn't run.

Murphy charged toward the cat, but when he arrived, Cheddar was still there. Murphy stopped, looked at the cat, then at me, confused. I advised him it was his dilemma, not mine. He turned back to his prey and jumped at him. No luck. Cheddar held his ground.

Finally, Murphy lowered his huge head and pushed the cat with his nose, as if to encourage him to get on with the game. The cat responded by laying down, his long tail twitching back and forth. Murphy stared at the cat for several seconds, then he lay down, extended his head and took the cat's neck in his mouth. I panicked and was about to yell at the hunter turned killer when I realized he was not applying any pressure to the cat's neck. The cat's paw was resting on Murphy's head, and his tail was playfully twitching.

Murphy took his mouth from Cheddar's throat and rolled over on top of the cat. Not deliberate I'm sure, but did I mention he weighed 95 pounds? Cheddar struggled out from under the beast, shook himself and lay back down beside, and touching the great hunter turned humanitarian. It was very embarrassing, but another ritual was created. From that moment forward, I would open the door each morning to let Murphy out and the cat would be perched in a chair just outside. On his way to the yard and the morning marking ritual, Murphy would gently grab Cheddar's neck, then release it and be on his way.

In his last year, Murphy would grab for the cat's neck and fall. He would get up, embarrassed, and the cat would have moved closer, as if to make it easier for the old hunter to try again. What a strange relationship these two old foes evolved; from opposites to tolerance to—dare I say it—friendship. Behavior most of us could probably work at improving.

   Murphy was doing what he was supposed to do by nature; chase a cat. But then with age and wisdom, maybe he decided the cat wasn't so bad after all, so he tempered his actions and ultimately discovered a new friend. Of course, it could be that if he had crunched the cat, there would be nothing to chase every morning. I choose to believe the former theory because the other explanation reeks of ulterior motives, and I know you will agree there are far too many of those around!

   I should add here that Cheddar was a very rough cat, lest I create an image of this big brute of a dog mauling a defenseless cat. I was the only person who could scratch his ear or stroke him without coming away bleeding; well, most of the time, anyway. I have to confess he did manage to get me a few times. Okay, more than a few times, but in fairness, I was as much at fault as he for the loss of blood on occasion. I deduced quickly and painfully that while this very large feline liked affection, he played rough. Because Murphy's playfulness rubbed off on me, the next natural step with Cheddar was a game. The game was simple; anytime I passed near the cat, I would try to pet him without getting mauled. This happened quite often because he caught on to the game and would move into my path anytime I approached, knowing the game was afoot. If I was in a hurry and tried to scoot around the yellow fur ball, a large paw would come snaking out and grab my jeans, or worse, in the summer, my bare leg. Murphy witnessed these events with interest and learned from my mistakes because if I got tagged, Murphy would change his direction following me and take the 'danger, bypass route' to the front door. He was a dog, but not a dumb dog.

Cheddar was tolerant of Murphy to the point of putting his life in jeopardy. Likewise, Murphy was tolerant of the cat even though he was jealous of my affection toward Cheddar. I think they both understood that in order to share the same space, compromises had to be made; a little give and take here and there. Like most of us ought to do more.

Murphy grieved when Cheddar died. For days afterward, as we came out the door for the morning rituals, he would stop and stare at the chair where Cheddar should have been perched. He would then look at me with those eyes that said so much. I explained the situation, and he seemed to understand. His eyes suggested he understood. Sometimes, in situations where logic simply will not or cannot do the job, we can believe what works for us. I chose to believe Murphy understood and accepted the situation. That's what worked for me.

No 'po mouth

Murphy was a great workout coach. I use the word coach because for the most part, coaches watch. They give encouragement, they use eye and body language to approve and disapprove, rather than actively participate. That's what Murphy did. Each time I would go into the room where my Bowflex and other instruments of torture were, Murphy would pad along behind me. He always sat in the same place, where he had a close and unobstructed view. If I were really into the workout session, he would lay down, still watching. If I got lazy, he would raise his head. If I needed motivation, I would talk to him and usually he would set up, become more attentive. This would oblige me to get off my duff and get with the program. I mean, for a dog to struggle from the prone to a sitting position—that has to be rewarded!

There were times I would have the TV on, and during the workout, when something on the tube caught my interest, I would stop to watch. Murphy would then change his position and look away from me as if he disapproved. The quiet coach. My interpretation of his movements guided my workouts. Some of his weird looks gave me brief, chuckling, respite from the physical rigors of the routine. It really worked well.

It's interesting what body language can tell us. We all use it. Some people are really good at interpreting body language. Some just think they are. Some take it to extremes. They study you, looking for tell-tell signs. It would be much easier if they just asked, instead of guessing. Communication is a wonderful thing. It informs, it clarifies, it answers. Some people just don't communicate very well. They don't say anything when they talk. Then there are those who, as my old southern bred ma would say, just 'po-mouth'. Loosely defined, that suggests those people complain about things that just don't matter, or can't be changed; like the weather, so why bother.

Murphy was a great communicator. Very direct and to the point. If he needed to go out, he went to the door. If he wanted on the couch with me, he walked over and placed his nose two inches from mine until I made room. If he needed a snack, he walked into the kitchen, put his nose to the floor, and circled and sniffed until a) I gave him a treat, or b) he gave up and returned to his bed with a disgusted glance. No games. No "What exactly does he mean." Very clear. We could learn from that. Word games are tiring. Witty conversation snippits are boring. Clear discussion is good. Murphy was a master at eliminating guesswork. Often the tilt of his head accompanied with tail wag would do the trick. Sometimes his attention wandered. When that happened he simply turned his attention to something else, usually a nap.

I was watching him one day as he studied a grasshopper. His nose a few inches from the insect, he watched it move through the grass, but every few seconds he would look away until finally, he yawned, rolled on his back, wiggled in the grass, then stretched out and dozed off. It seemed so simple. How did he do that? There are times when I give my attention to something, like Murphy studying a bug, but my mind wanders. Unlike Murphy, I don't roll in the grass and go to sleep; I force my mind to stay with the situation even though it obviously doesn't want to be in the situation. In retrospect, I like Murphy's way better.

Take out and dine at home

Murphy was not always a good dog. There were times when either by an act or an omission, he did not please me. This was particularly true in his younger years. Dogs, like us, do tend to mellow with age, but Murphy did try my patience before he hit that stage. His ability as the great escape artist, for example.

During the years Murphy enjoyed the status of backyard river dog, he passed his time with Tiffer in a grassy, spacious yard, bordered at the end by the wonderful St. Johns River and on the sides by a four foot high fence. He loved the yard, snoozing in a lovely breeze on the dock, or perched on top of the picnic table, where he had a higher vantage point of the sights and sounds of his world. I think I mentioned he liked to run. Well, he particularly enjoyed running outside the yard; thru the woods, neighbors yards, the road—you get the picture. So he did that. Often. Before these outside perimeter forays, his limbering exercise included jumping the fence. Concerned about his welfare, I extended the fence higher. Not high enough. Undaunted by this miscalculation, I then erected a six foot privacy fence along both sides and the front, with a six foot chain link gate. All this new construction went in front of a perfectly good chain link fence. He was not a cheap dog. The fence worked. He couldn't jump it. The gate didn't work; he climbed it. Six feet high! So I made the gate climb proof.

This was getting to be quite a lot of work and expense, but at least now he couldn't go over the top. The ever resourceful Murphy dog took the next logical step; he went under. That beast had at least a size 12 set of feet, ninety five pounds of muscle and was a digging fool. He was an excavator, backhoe, and dirt spreader all rolled up in one determined body. I finally cemented under the fence, and I did it with sinister glee; I would not be outdone by this overgrown brute of a dog. That's the way we are when our pride is injured. Work and expense became irrelevant. It became personal. Human versus dog. I would prevail! And I did. Peace and harmony returned to the backyard and in the neighborhood.

Sometimes, unexpected events can fall out of the strangest situations. A fallout of Murphy's outside the fence adventures was our introduction to neighbors we had not met before.

One such couple called one afternoon to ask if I had a large brown and white speckled dog with large ears. When I answered in the affirmative, she calmly said, "Well, he's currently dragging our large, full garbage bag down the road toward your house." "He should be in the backyard," I replied, knowing even as I uttered the words, he probably was not. A glance through the window verified this.

As in most cases, there were positive aspects to this situation. The beast didn't choose to rip the bag of garbage open, preferring instead to do take out and dine at home, and we subsequently became good friends with the neighbors, whom we had not previously met.

Murphy felt bad. I could always tell because his very long ears drooped even lower and he wouldn't look at me; he did that when his conscience bothered him. Kinda like us. His pathetic demeanor helped defuse the situation which could have easily turned into a yelling, defensive contest. People do that over such mundane things. In this case, however, I made Murphy accompany me when I went to offer my apologies. I scolded him all the way to the neighbors house, and by the time we arrived he looked so pathetic that even a cynic couldn't be angry.

The lady was formal and reserved initially, eyeballing the beast with distain. Then she blew it. She touched his pathetically drooping, soft head. He didn't lick her—Murphy didn't lick. But he did sigh and put his nose on her hand. She laughed and muttered "you poor thing". Situation resolved. The power of the Murphy dog prevailing against all odds.

Salutations, sniffing, and noisy things

Murphy was what you would call a quiet dog. He seldom barked, and when he did, it was usually associated with play, and if he barked when at play, he was really having a great time. When we were in the yard and someone approached, he would "alert"; a form of posturing, but gracefully—well, as graceful as you can be when you have really large ears and look kinda funny. After a quick sniff and my acknowledgement of the visitor's presence, Murphy would move on to other endeavors, like lizards, frogs, and such. The only exception I can recall to this behavior was the "gate man case".

The gate man was a fellow with whom I had arranged to meet at my place to discuss a gate project. When he arrived, Murphy and I were standing inside the old gate contemplating the project. The fellow stopped his truck on the other side of the gate and approached us. Murphy went nuts. He began growling, and when the gate guy spoke and extended his hand over the gate to the beast, Murphy went after him aggressively. I was shocked and embarrassed—and worried. I had to physically restrain the dog I thought I knew. Murphy did not like this fellow, and that should have told me something. When it became obvious the beast was not going to calm down, I took him to the house, secured him, and issued a stern scolding.

I returned to the front and gave the gate guy a deposit check for work agreed to, along with my apology for Murphy's behavior. When he left, I returned to the house, very angry, to deal with Murphy. When I opened the door, he charged out, ran down the driveway like a beast possessed and stopped at the gate, growling. I was, to say the least, astounded. Murphy's behavior was totally out of character. He finally settled down, I finally settled down, and things returned to normal, except for the gate deal. I never saw or heard from the guy again—except for my cancelled check which he had promptly cashed. My research revealed he had ripped off several people in the area. That old instinct thing again.

Obviously, Murphy's instinct was "don't trust this guy". Equally obvious was my failure to use good instinct. I had to apologize to Murphy. He grudgingly accepted with an 'I told you so' look. My bad instincts cost me two apologies, three hundred bucks and a gate still broken.

I should have paid attention to Murphy. I knew him, I could have read his signals. I just blew it. I should have known his aggressive behavior meant something. He never even got aggressive with other dogs, unless forced to. His usual demeanor when another dog approached was one of alert curiosity, followed by the obligatory sniff.

The sniff. I concluded long ago that dog sniffing is a form of salutation. It's a fraternity. When I ride my cycle down highway 13 along the river and another cycle approaches, we each drop our left hand out and down in greeting. Not a wave, but a casual acknowledgement. A fellow cycle rider acknowledgement. It's a fraternity. Like sniffing. Two male dogs, upon meeting, will at some point sniff each other. They're a fraternity, and sniffing is the salutation. The sniffing is preceded by posturing. They never immediately sniff. They posture first. It's a rule. A fraternal rule. Like the cycle signal. It has to be—just so-cool, suave, in control, a sign that we know the secret. That's part of the rule. The fraternal rule. I'm good at it, but my salutation paled when compared to the Murphy dog.

He was the king preener and sniffer. Ears up [top part only], tail erect, a blur in its movement. He humbled the other guy, uh, dog, and he didn't make noise like most of the other sniffers. His actions and demeanor spoke for him. Clint Eastwoodish—strong, quiet—a man of few words because words weren't necessary.

I enjoy people who are like Murphy—not the sniffing, but quieter, not loud. People who speak with action and don't make noise, talk loud or do other obnoxious things. Like horn blowing. Some people will blow their car horn at every opportunity, and most of the time it has nothing to do with safety—it's being a jerk. Like dogs that bark at everything and everyone who walk by their fence. Same thing. Why? I forgive the dog—he's probably bored; but the horn blowers...not so much. The local folks who blow their horns at tourists because they are moving too slow are particularly annoying. I mean, they're tourists! They are in town to tour the nation's oldest city—our city. Give them a break. Tacky behavior. I have every confidence that had Murphy known about horn blowing, those folks would have gotten the same treatment as the gate guy. Guaranteed.

Rules vs. guidelines

We are bound to rules in every facet of life. History has shown that man needs rules. Without them, we don't seem to do well. Aggravating on occasion. Who has not encountered those situations where you feel a rule should not apply; there should be an exception. Murphy lived in those predicaments; they were his norm. He had rules—my rules—but he either didn't know that, or he ignored them when he chose. He viewed rules as guidelines. If the rule didn't interfere with his current endeavor or desire, he followed it. If it was not convenient, or to his liking, he did not. The rule became a guide only. I knew the rules and they seemed simple enough, but the beast appeared to have other views. Try as I might, I could never accept that—well, almost never. If he violated a simple rule, or the situation dictated a judgment call to allow an exception, I let him slide. He appreciated that. I could tell because with some rule violations, my immediate scornful voice made it clear he had screwed up. But with my subsequent forgiving tone, I would get the wiggle and nose touch. He probably never knew what all that was about. I enjoyed forgiving him, but there was sometimes an ulterior motive.

So many times in my life I felt I should have been granted a rule exception but didn't get it. It's fun to exercise judgment in deciding to punish or not when you decide not. To give another chance. I enjoyed doing that with Murphy because I recall a time, in years past, when the world was a kinder, gentler place. When a cop would give you a stern lecture and send you on your way; when you could peek through the fence to see a ball game if you couldn't pay, without getting arrested; when neighbors would call parents and not the police when kids misbehaved; when discussions resolved issues, before lawyers took over.

Murphy's mind was not muddled with 'should I or should I not.' If he even understood that rule infractions were followed by punishment, he obviously didn't care or probably more accurate, he knew punishment would be no big deal and short-lived. You have to envy him that freedom. My mother's punishment when my brother and I acted up was never physical—no spanking—and could be negotiated. My father, not so much. To Murphy, when punishment was involved, I was his mother.

Maybe he knew I didn't have the heart to 'man-up' and dole out swift, harsh punishment.

I do suspect Murphy knew I would not be harsh and that I would forgive him. I suspect that because he always immediately forgave me when I screwed up, it followed that he knew I would reciprocate. Dog logic. It rubs off. It causes fresh perspective. It makes you feel good, and jealous. Jealous because I feel, as everyone should, that it is our manifest destiny to do as we please, with due consideration to others, of course. Now, even though rules, both social and otherwise can interfere with that pursuit at times, we can think it through, exercise alternate routes to at least come close to that quest. Murphy had the gift of spontaneity. He acted as he pleased. If I hampered a particular endeavor with rules and he could not easily convert the rule to a guide, he simply shifted gears and did something else that pleased him. The essence of win-win, without planning, without thought. Just did it. Didn't dwell on the obstacle depriving him of a certain act—just go to the next act.

He didn't even have to learn that and he certainly didn't think about whether or not he was violating a rule, he just did it until he found one he could ignore and get away unscathed. He wore me down. I either forgave him or gave up. Same end result for him. Now that's manifest destiny.

My hands were tied. I couldn't ground him—he would just take a nap. I couldn't put him on bread and water because he loved bread. I certainly couldn't hit him—that would violate our pact. I could only speak in a disapproving tone and that was worthless because I couldn't do it and walk away. He melted me. He knew it. My hands were tied, my feet were tied. My heart was his property, and he used that knowledge to achieve his own manifest destiny without even knowing what the concept was.

Drywall does not taste good

I recall when my sons were younger, they didn't listen very well; or, maybe they listened but didn't heed the sage advice or directions being put forth. Now that I think about it, maybe I was the same way once upon a time. So was Murphy.

Between the ages of perhaps three and seven, there were times he made me crazy, to say the least. I have to confess that years after the fact, many of those frustrating or anger provoking antics are really funny. Not all, though. Chewing about two square feet of drywall off the wall—not so funny. I haven't thought about that in years, and now that I have, it occurs to me that after that incident, he never chewed anything else. I know why. It just hit me. IT'S DRYWALL! One-half inch wallboard; chalky, dusty, yucky drywall. It had to taste terrible. The question that begs to be asked is why did he chew out such a large portion if it tasted so bad? Of course, I never viewed the Murphy dog as logical anyway. Wow! I have a mental picture of Murphy ripping off a chunk, chewing, with plaster flying, the dry, tasteless material sticking to his wet tongue and mouth, as it surely must have. But, he kept at it. Two feet.

I've done that. Probably everyone has. Engaging in some activity, then becoming aware it isn't very pleasant, but continuing anyway. Usually though, we don't repeat the process if we found it distasteful, but not always.

Murphy must have found this chewing episode very unpleasant. Think about it; drywall, powder, saliva, clay; what a combination. But then, no more chewing on things not his own. If only we could all correct our mistakes after only one bad episode. We don't, of course. If a dog, even Murphy, does something we regard as stupid, our view probably is, "Hey, he's a dog." If he does it again, same view. Understanding, acceptance, maybe even forgiveness. Not so much with humans. Sometimes it's hard to understand, harder even to forgive. We do it with dogs; they do it with us. But we sometimes don't do it with each other. Even stupid little things. Not important, not significant, not worth re-visiting, but still, we dwell on them, or we seek revenge over stupid actions caused by stupid situations—like standing in line.

We spend a lot of time in lines throughout our lives. Much of that "line time" we don't want to be there so things happen, perhaps out of aggravation. I was in the vehicle tag line (you know, the take a number deal) last week—way back—when I observed an interesting situation. Two guys in line were talking, and as the line progressed forward, a small gap between them and the person in front of them would open because they were unaware the line had moved, so engrossed were they in conversation. No big deal because it was a long line. The gentleman behind them however was bothered by this action and each time they failed to move promptly when the line moved, he cleared his throat to register his disapproval—the talkers would then move, but only after a disapproving glance. After the third 'throat clearing', one of the talkers looked at the culprit and stated, "If you do that one more time, I'm gonna pull that frog out of your throat." I believe you might call that a slight overreaction to a simple situation.

I have to blame the throat clearer for precipitating the incident because it was clear who was where in this very orderly line. He would have been better off using one of Murphy's tricks when boredom set in—lay down and sleep.

We really do need to exercise more patience and not allow ourselves to get agitated over stupid stuff. Act like a dog. Ask yourself, "What would my dog do in this situation?" Minor adjustments may have to be made to make the 'man vs. dog behavior regarding what is allowed' transition—I mean I wouldn't recommend you mark a bush or chair as your dog might, but the thought process would do wonders for you. Trust me on this; I do it all the time and it seldom fails to cause me to smile when I imagine what the beast might do.

Reality

Before I turned the living room light off last night, I glanced at the couch to check Murphy. He wasn't there. I think I heard his breathing. I also looked at the space where his bed had been; I had finally moved it out. This morning on the way out, headed to the Old Town, I noted the water level in his dish was the same. No, I haven't moved it yet. I will eventually. The trip to St. George Street will be a break.

Pee-wee dogs and valor

I took Murphy to St. George Street several years ago. It didn't work out too well. It took about three trips to come to that conclusion. The problem wasn't really Murphy; well, in a way.

St. George is in the heart of old historic St. Augustine. No vehicles allowed. Pedestrians only and lots of 'em. It is after all a tourist town. I park at the opposite end of St. George when I have business at the other end of the street so I can stroll; say hello to shop owner friends; watch the tourists. I love people watching. Those few times I took Murphy, I followed this same habit, knowing Murphy was very good on leash, an attribute not shared by many dogs I see. But, here was the problem; a two-fold problem: 1) people can't keep their hands off Murphy. That head. Think about that. People run up to small, cutesy dogs to pet and carry-on all the time. How many people run up to a big, ninety-five pound beast with size twelve feet? Well, they did with Murphy. Same thing when we ran on Vilano Beach. Think about what I am saying. The last time you passed a very large, and, okay, ugly dog that you didn't know, did you reach your hand out? I suspect not. Well, you probably would if it were Murphy, and he would soak it up until you had your fill.

Second problem: Lots of tourists have dogs with them. Thousands. And they're all small. All small dogs bark at Murphy. I have never witnessed a small dog who did not bark at Murphy. In fifteen years. Some people are like that about some things. They bark at you, in a fashion.

Barking cannot have a positive outcome if you're human. I know some folks I should remind of that from time to time. But then again, maybe not.

Anyway, Murphy's reaction to this phenomenon is consistent, predictable, reliable. He stops, goes rigid, stares intently, but does not bark or growl back. It's spooky. I would take in the leash and tighten my grip as I felt his muscled body tighten, the power flowing up the leash. He could have lunged and taken my arm with him. But he never did. He never moved. Most people would keep their pups well away. Others I would need to caution to do that, just in case. All those times and Murphy never offered to go after a small dog, never acted aggressive. I don't know if it was because I was holding the leash and talking to him, or if it was just his nature. Maybe both. I don't know, but I was always grateful for his response. After all, some of those small breeds would be like one of those giant dog bones I used to give Murphy. He ate drywall for goodness sake!

Those were the two problems with Murphy and St. George Street; petting and pee-wee dogs. Both situations involved stopping; not moving forward toward the destination at the other end of the street. So Murphy went many places with me, but not St. George Street. In the few times he did go though, I realize I learned, or was reminded of some things, thanks in part to his behavior. Not the petting part; he was always a ham. The small dog part...Tolerance, discipline, demeanor. Nothing good would have come from him crunching one of those dogs, or even scaring the crap out of them. So, he didn't do it.

Now, you may be thinking that Murphy gave these situations calm, logical thought and decided that discretion was the better part of valor. I'm not saying that at all. Well, maybe I am. Don't really know, but I do know that we all would be well served to exercise that kind of control and demeanor in precarious situations. We sometimes don't though we wish we had after the fact. Murphy always did that and he was just a dog.

Alien beasts and panhandlers

Murphy enjoyed downtown and the attention he received—though there was the alien dog affair. One of the few occasions Murphy was barkless (dog speak for speechless).

The alien was a dog, hound variety, clad in a coat with King George ruffles, a derby hat, and large sunglasses. The dog half of a man and dog scam team. They were walking toward us and as we were about to pass, Murphy and the derby hound stopped and eyeballed each other. The encounter was completely non-aggressive except for Murphy's big eyes.

In similar situations, the Murphy dog might have approached and sniffed, or simply walked away. This time, his feet were frozen to the pavement and his expression was...suitable for framing in a picture. A look that said, "What the hell...," or " Are you kidding me?" Or maybe, "What are you thinking?" he was dumbfounded. Can dogs be dumbfounded? I think Murphy was.

Murphy saw a variety of 'different' people downtown, many dressed in strange garbs. People with green hair, with stuffed creatures clinging to their backs; many displaying strange behavior. Never bothered him. Never even interested him that much. But this eye shaded mutt obviously confused his senses. Personally, I thought the owner looked more strange, but then my perspective and Murphy's regarding visual stimuli were sometimes different. Visual perception varies greatly among we humans too. During art walk downtown, I have watched people gaga over a piece of art which to me was a "You can't be serious," situation, (yeah, to each his own), like Murphy with his new acquaintance.

Ultimately, the derby hound and his owner strolled away. I held Murphy's leash loose in my hand because I was curious to see what the beast would do. He watched the dog walk away, then looked around the street, as if searching for other aliens. Finally, he looked up at me as if searching for direction, or perhaps an explanation. I said the first thing that came to mind, "Would you like a hat?" The beast lifted his ears (top part only), turned, and proceeded down the street, away from the other dog, at a brisk pace. I interpreted this to mean, "You can't be serious!" We thought alike in many cases.

Though this was the Murphy dog's first encounter with this dog, I had seen his owner and him several times before. The owner was a panhandler. Loosely defined as folks who ask other folks for money, usually without reciprocation; unless you count taking a picture of the dog.

There seems to be an inordinate number of people who panhandle in historic downtown St. Augustine. They wander about asking for change, and in some cases, disrupting passersby who are enjoying the Old Town. It seems to me that unless you truly need help or you are a stray cat or dog, you should not panhandle.

Murphy, like most dogs, was a panhandler. He panhandled for food, a scratch, a walk, a spot on the couch. But he reciprocated in his own way. Panhandling is OK in some situations. Murphy's reasons were legitimate and so are folks who honestly can't make their own way, like homeless people with mental issues. Usually those are older individuals and they need help. Younger panhandlers bother me. Most of those I encountered appear sane—so sane they try to impress you with their wit and logic regarding a handout. That's no good. It isn't right to inflict yourself on others by interrupting their leisurely pursuits with scam verbage and behavior.

I yielded to Murphy's panhandling because that was the arrangement. He was confined to the house and yard and couldn't fend for himself because I controlled his environment. If I had released him to the woods, he would have survived because he possessed the abilities to do that. If younger panhandlers who can work didn't get money by begging, would they change their behavior and actually work? If they enjoyed eating, probably so.

I frequently raid the kitchen for a snack. Murphy was familiar with this exercise and would be close on my heels, looking to mooch. He couldn't get his own snack because they were in a cabinet. He had to panhandle, and was very good at it. A legitimate form of panhandling. While I support our youth pursuing their own freedom of expressions while 'finding themselves', they shouldn't do it by being a leech. In the words of Clint Eastwood in the movie, 'Gran Torino', "man up."

The man room, bluffing, and dog jobs

I tolerated more than a few of Murphy's antics, but I suspect he tolerated a lot more of mine. Like disturbing his blissful nap in the man room during my various vocal thinking sessions.

Murphy was the only living thing authorized routine access into the man room. Named by my wife, the man room is my place of reflection, of ranting, of solitude. It's where I write. A crude, primitive (according to some), room built over the workshop by yours truly. A place full of stuff. Important stuff, but only to me, and I usually can't find any of it. It's where ideas fly into my face with a whack as I stare out at the river or the wall or at Murphy snoozing on his bed (yeah, he had one up there, too). It's my place. Murphy's place. Our place. Never mind that no one else would want it; it was ours.

Countless times, as we were finishing some chore in the yard, or just wandering around in the grass, Murphy would walk to the stairs leading up to the man room and look up. Then he would look at me. A Murphy signal: "Let's go up to the man room". It always seemed like a good idea, so we usually did.

When one of my sons or my brother would visit, we'd go to the man room to chat; they being the rare visitors allowed access. Murphy joined us but most of the time he would not doze. He liked those guys and they him, but nevertheless he stayed alert, looking from me to them as we spoke. Normally, when I spoke in the man room, it was to Murphy. He was the only one present. I think it might be that with someone else there, he wasn't sure whether I was speaking to him or the other person. No doubt he regarded them as intruders. I say this because if we were all in the house or on the dock, Murphy would be snoozing, his normal position. Sometimes we're like that. We don't want to miss anything, or maybe in a way we're protecting territory.

There were nine steps going up to the man room. For years, Murphy would bolt by me going up. I figured he didn't want me to beat him to his bed. Over the past year, he went up much slower, until finally, I had to assist him. I finally put a gate at the entrance after he tried to go up on his own and only made it half way when he tumbled down. He was embarrassed but uninjured and promptly started up again, this time with my assistance. After all, there's no need to stop doing something you enjoy because of some obstacle. There's always a way to make adjustments and keep truckin'.

I considered making a long wheelchair ramp affair for the fool, but abandoned that idea when I had to confess that he would just lay on the ramp to catch the afternoon sun and get sunburned.

The man room is my writing place. It is where I create and capture great ideas and some not so great. I wad and toss lots of paper. Murphy became my blank slate which, as I stared at his snoozing body, became full. He was a sounding board, though often reluctant-or unaware. I read things to him so we could hear how it sounded. He was required to be awake in order to participate, so when necessary, I woke him. The criterion I established for the beast was simple: If my reading or thoughts put him to sleep, it apparently was not very good. If he remained attentive, probably okay.

That system seemed simple enough to me, but Murphy often didn't seem to take the arrangement seriously enough. For whatever reason though, it did seem to help me, even when I ignored his response when it was not to my liking. There was an exception. If he actually got up and walked to the door during my reading, I threw the work away. My logic was that if the piece was so bad it caused the beast to flee, the words weren't worth keeping. Dogs sense things and even though Murphy couldn't read, I think the rhythmic sound of words pleased him, unless the melody was flawed. I recall only one time that turned out to not be the case. In that instance, I retrieved the wadded up passage—it was wonderful—and counseled Murphy to pay more careful attention. He did, though some prodding was still required.

One time, to ensure he took his job seriously, I threatened to ban him from the man room. I was bluffing, but he didn't know it. Bluffing is okay sometimes, in some situations, with some people, but only if warranted and you understand and are willing to accept the consequences if the bluff fails. I don't think Murphy considered part two. He bluffed all the time but seemed totally uncooperative relative to the consequences if he failed. But, he was a great listener.

Most of us could better learn and practice the art of listening by taking cues from our dogs. We don't listen well. In my case, it's because I'm sometimes too impatient. Instead of listening, enjoying the exchange, my mind slips into never-never land.

Murphy watched intently as I spoke. It made me feel good even though he may or may not have understood what I was saying. It didn't matter because it made me feel good.

I miss talking to the Murphy dog. His demeanor encouraged my free expression. He would listen patiently to my most profound discussions, though many times my ranting would meander. He didn't seem to mind, and if he did, he might shift his position slightly. Thus, never a verbal interruption. People pay shrinks for the opportunity to do that— to verbally release or mind wander. My shrink was free, except for the occasional scratch. Tit for tat.

There were times when I was so rejuvenated upon completion of my brain cell renewal session, I would jump up and state to the beast, "Up and at 'em." He would likewise jump up, bark, and run to the door. Could be he was relieved the session was over, but probably it was because he was happy I felt better. Perception is important. That's why I choose to believe the latter. That's the good thing about perceptions. We get to pick. Infrequently I wished he could verbally respond, but most of the time, not. I always felt he understood and his silence was a verification of that. It's nice when we can choose to believe what we will, without argument or lengthy encounters. It's clean and easy on the head.

Lab rat and thinking about stuff

Murphy was my bud. We rolled in the grass together. We ran and walked together. We frolicked in the river together—well, I frolicked, he hunted fish. We hung out in the man room. We did everything together. We enjoyed each other, but I had a dark secret Murphy was oblivious to—I used him as a lab rat.

It was a game. I would try to predict his behavior in various situations, or understand his behavior. A fascinating endeavor. I would change things to cause him to break a routine to see what would happen. For instance, when we went up to the man room, his behavior was very predictable. He would walk in, sniff (to ensure no aliens had preceded us), walk to his bed, do the circle thing and lay down. If I were in my scientist mode, I would leave him on the outside stoop, go in, shut the door and sit down. He would stare through the glass door at me for twenty two seconds, give or take, then lay down on the landing. Every time. Never went back down the stairs, never whimpered—though he did give me disgusted looks every now and then. Very predictable.

Other times, I would leave him out, go in, and move his bed across the room, then let him in. He wouldn't walk to the bed at its new location. Instead, he would walk to where it was supposed to be. He would then sniff the floor, scratch at it lightly, probably to verify the bed's absence, then do the circle thing and lay down. Now, here's the thing; he would always lay with his head on his paws, looking directly at me. If I did or said nothing for about one minute, he would get up, walk to the bed at its' new location, look at me again, and lay down—no circles—just lay straight down on the bed. I theorized that the reason for no pre-lay circles was a) he was confused and had already wasted enough nap time, or b), and more likely, he was trying to confuse me. He did, and I'll never know for sure.

Lab rat. I conducted many experiments with the beast and fortunately, he always displayed a patient attitude, not unlike I always tried to do with my sons when they were doing something weird. Wait a minute. Maybe Murphy viewed me as a child being weird, and it was he who was the wise, patient adult. Satre once said, "The more sand has escaped from the hourglass of our life, the clearer we should see through it." That was definitely true of Murphy in his later years. In his wisdom, he simply accepted with patience, and adapted.

I watch people too. Most writers do. You learn things, imagine things. We, like Murphy, are often predictable, and we really do follow the lead of others often. Like dogs, we do that. If one dog does something, others around him will usually follow suit. I was recently honored to have one of my books selected as a finalist in the Eric Hoffer Book Awards. A great American philosopher and novelist, Eric Hoffer. He said that "When people are free to do as they please, they usually imitate each other." For the most part, I have found that to be true. Dogs do that because they just act without much thinking. Wonder why we do it? I could theorize about conditioning and all that, but I'll spare you. Besides, it's all just a wonderful game, watching people. Murphy played games, I played games. I played more when he came along because it was obvious that he must be on to something. I mean, he had so much fun. People became my lizards and frogs. Murphy was my professor and unknowing mentor. He caused me to think about things.

It is fun to think about stuff that means...nothing. Like why my generation called that fine smelling beach oil sun tan lotion, and now we call it sunscreen. I put sunscreen on Murphy's nose when we were out for extended periods. He would lick most of it off, and he seemed to like it; I believe his personal favorite was that coconut smelling stuff.

I think about things. Things like why grocery stores move the older stuff to the front and newer stuff to the back, particularly items like milk and eggs. Who does not reach to the back to get the freshest stuff? I don't know why they even bother.

I tried to 'rotate stock' with Murphy, but it didn't work. For instance, sometimes I would give him a dog bone and if he didn't want it right away (this rarely happened), he would drop it on the floor. If I forgot and gave him another bone a short time later, he would do likewise. When I realized he now had two bones on the floor, I rotated the oldest one to the front, at which time he panicked, charged to the bone stash and ate both. So much for rotation.

It's fun to think about stupid things. Like why, every time I need to mow the grass, I debate whether to use the riding mower or the push mower first. I need to use both because the push mower will go between the bushes and do the close in perimeter work. Doesn't matter which I do first.

Same result. Murphy didn't care either because after I cut the grass, particularly around bushes, he re-marked all of them—some of the less hearty varieties of plants died; he was like a walking Roundup weed killer. He didn't care if I rode first, or walked; same procedure for him. But I always debated it. Even flipped a coin on occasion to decide which to do first, and based on the look I got from Murphy when I did this, it is very fortunate none of my neighbors saw me. Crazy, but I think about things. I thought, Murphy marked.

I always wondered why Murphy, and most dogs, sniffed the entire yard before picking a place to do the 'big job'. I never did develop a reasonable theory. By the way, Murphy was not one of those 'one spotters' when he did the job. Oh no. Murphy moved forward as the job progressed, so the scooping (that would be me) involved two, three, or even four bend and scoops. He would watch me, as if deciding whether or not to approve my scoop technique. Did he regard me as his housekeeper? I think about things—sometimes too much. Sometimes, my head gets too full.

I mute the television during commercials. Drives my wife crazy. Confused Murphy. If he were snoozing and the TV was on, he'd wake up when I muted it and look around like, "What changed?" Can dogs hear while they're sleeping?

I started the muting thing because I determined that many of the commercials were driving me insane. Many times politicians have that effect on me, but that's easy—I don't watch. If you watch a program on commercial TV however, you're stuck with commercials. They turned me into Mr. Hyde. I said things, out loud, in response—with no one else in the room except Murphy, and he began taking some of my comments personally. Because no one else was around, he thought I was talking to him. The final straw was an outburst I unconsciously used frequently, usually in response to an absolutely ridiculous claim. "You're lying like a dog!" I would yell. Oh, the look I would get from the beast. He even whimpered if he was having one of his more sensitive days. I broke myself when I realized the situation—for him to even speculate that I was calling him a dog—well, I couldn't bear it.

I think about stuff and my head gets full. Murphy didn't think, so his head was pretty much empty. A lady, Sue Murphy, once said, "Did you ever walk into a room and forget why you walked in? I think that is how dogs spend their lives."

There you have it. In those two sentences, Sue captured the essence of a dog. The joy of being a dog. The empty head syndrome—the idea seems to have merit.

Blackmail, the creation of a ham, and flatulence

You can learn a lot talking to a dog, but you can't be cute about it. You must verbalize, just as you would with another person. A discussion, except you get to do all the talking. It's amazing what you can solve, learn, sort out, during that process. Now, it does help if the dog responds. Murphy would furrow his eyebrows or lift his ears (top part only because the rest was to long and heavy), and, unfortunately, sometimes yawn. Since I was doing all the talking in these sessions, it didn't really matter what he did. That's what sounding boards are for. One time he yawned in the middle of my noteworthy discussion, promptly stood up, walked off the dock into the yard and marked a bush. This is a great example of why discussions with dogs are good—they humble you!

I seemed to get inspired when, in the silence of the man room, I could hear the ceiling fan and Murphy's soft breathing. He was my writing crutch, and he wasn't scratchy like a rabbit's foot. It's okay to have little things, even silly little things, that motivate us, even if we're the only one who understands; that makes it even more meaningful. That 'little thing' to me was the Murphy dog. I did reward him for this arrangement by giving him bit parts in some of my books. He liked it, but he got greedy.

People would ask about him at book signings. I made the mistake of telling him, and he wanted more, so like an idiot, I included his picture with me on the 'about the author' pages in my books. He liked that even more, but it made him far too popular. As a two-bit author, I'm flattered when someone shows an interest in my book. More-so when they ask me to sign it and talk about the story. I enjoyed that, at least before the ham got his picture in the act.

Now, eight out of ten people don't even ask about the story. They ask about the beautiful pointer. Beautiful pointer! Brother! I didn't tell Murphy about this phenomenon, but he seemed to know. He was a spoiled celebrity. It was almost to much too handle. This beast weaseled his way into the house; his doghouse out back grew cobwebs. He took half the floor with his bed; his expensive bed. Was that enough? No, he took my couch. He caused me to put steps (book boxes) at the foot of my bed so he could get his old, stiff body all over me when I was trying to relax or read. He owned me, but I needed him. He sold books. He developed a following. It was like blackmail. A wonderful blackmail.

There are a lot of people who enjoy talking about animals, particularly dogs. They asked, I told. I have messed up more than a few books trying to sign my name while regaling a crowd with Murphy stories.

They would laugh as I described his white face, which was at one time brown, covered with chocolate from the three-pound sampler box I inadvertently left out and he promptly ate. Three pounds! Because I left it right beside him, he obviously viewed it as a gift. What a commercial that face would have made. Like coming home and finding a young kid smeared with candy because the temptation was too much to resist. That episode did scare me. Three pounds!

I called the vet and was informed that dogs have died from ingesting chocolate, even small amounts. She gave explicit instructions. If certain things happened, bring the beast in immediately. We stayed up all night, checking pupils, temperature, responsiveness. He loved it. It was like an all night pajama party. The next morning the beast awoke refreshed and hungry. It was, after all, time for breakfast. I didn't awake because I had not slept. We walked the yard and I watched him do the perimeter check; the marking. Everything appeared normal so I called my report to the vet who stated that Murphy obviously had a cast iron stomach. Then she laughed and said she wasn't surprised. She laughed! But then, she had not been up all night.

I couldn't get angry at him, in part because I was conditioned to some degree. Murphy had, after all, over the years consumed entire bags of potato chips, boxes of donuts, and oh yes, a good sized bag of pistachio nuts as well as an assortment of other morsels left on the table or countertop. So I didn't get angry, though at first I was very worried. I was too tired to get angry, then I was too relieved, and finally, I was laughing too hard. If only I had taken a picture of that chocolate covered face. It's in my mind, though, and probably always will be. There does remain a question regarding that caper: Where did all those little candy wrapper cups go? You know, the little crinkled ones the candy sits in, two tiers of them. I counted at the vet's request, and as far as I could determine, several were gone. Cast iron stomach.

As I recall, after I let Murphy back inside that morning, I went back to the bedroom to stretch out for a few minutes. It had, after all been a long night. As usual, the beast followed me back, and with the aid of his bed steps, beat me to the bed. Good timing.   I needed to relax and I had discovered some years before when Murphy chilled out, it was easier for me to follow suit. Karma. Before, I would try various methods to relax. You know, breath in, breath out, focus your mind, or spirit, or whatever, and so on.   But Murphy stretched out and embodied the essence of relaxation, so that relaxed me, especially if we were touching. I could relax anytime I wanted because Murphy relaxed all the time so there was no planning required. There was a major trade-off.

Murphy often suffered from flatulence. Well, more than often, and he didn't suffer; I suffered. He was a master. One of my sons called him the "master gasser." I suppose most things in life are give and take or perhaps more appropriately, receive. Sometimes though, as in this case, the receive part may be a tad more than one might like, but in the Murphy-Randy relationship there were no facades given to protect the real person, or dog. The down side of that was that Murphy took the concept literally, in all situations, whether couth or uncouth. In the end, with unvarnished friendship, things probably even out.

"stop it, you're hurting my ears"

I was in the man room writing these few pages, and now I'm on the dock, staring at the ramp Murphy walked down into the water on countless occasions. The great fish hunter. How he loved it. There were times I couldn't let him go down; water too high, a little cold. He didn't understand, and he didn't like it. His reaction was always predictable; he would bark, and when that didn't work, he would sit down and make the twill noise, as if too drown out my explanation; words he didn't want to hear. It reminded me of one of my sons when he was nine or ten and I would be explaining why he couldn't do or have something. He would clasp both hands over his ears and yell, "stop it, you're hurting my ears." I think that's what Murphy was doing.

There are times I wish I could do that. You know, when a person is going on and on, or the words I'm hearing are not to my liking, so I just want them to go away. "Stop it, you're hurting my ears." I may try that the next time a salesperson is trying to explain why an item marked 19.95 is really 26.95. Probably won't work, but I'd love to see the guy's expression.

We can't always do what we want to do. It would be nice if we could. But, like Murphy, that doesn't mean we should quit trying. It's one of those phrases that's so overused, we don't pay attention, though it's true and appropriate. Sometimes we should go ahead and do something anyway, contrary to the words or advice we're hearing. There doesn't always need to be a reason, though it is good to have a reason. Like the Murphy dog, it's sometimes okay to do a thing…just because…

Murphy didn't understand the concept of failure. He would try some things repeatedly and never succeed. Like the sand pipers on Vilano Beach. I wish I had taken him to Vilano more during the past weeks. We used to go often. He would charge down the beach, just at the surf line, chasing those little birds whose feet move so fast they're only a blur. He never came close to catching one, but I suppose he thought he would one day. He was a good example for youngsters starting out. Keep trying, and perhaps more important, enjoy the trying. We talk about subjects such as that at Buddy Boy's during Porch Hog meetings.

Porch hogs...life is not simple

I was tempted many times to let Murphy accompany me to Buddy Boys, but usually I rode my cycle and I couldn't figure out a way to get the beast on it. He would have looked good, though. It is easy to visualize his sagging jowls and ears blowing in the breeze—or more likely, pounding against my helmet face shield.

Buddy Boys Country Store is two miles from my house. It's a real country store. Log cabin style, old, large front porch with well worn wood chairs. Gas, beer, ice, fish bait—you name it, they have it. Great coffee, and about sixty-five percent cheaper than that upscale place—you know the one I refer to.

Chickens loiter in the parking area looking for handouts. All manner of folks go there: boaters; construction workers; farm hands; yuppies; high income; low income; and Porch Hogs.

The Porch Hogs are a group of retired guys with cycles who gang up at Buddy Boys several mornings a week. Good way to start the day. We named ourselves. Porch Hogs kinda fit all those Harley's (some, including me, ride other make cycles, though we were all accepted in after some soul searching by the purists) and the overall demeanor of the place. Even have a logo. My good friend Billy designed it. Picture if you will a ruffian looking wild boar in a leather jacket with patches, a ring in his nose, sitting on a cycle. A laminated copy is posted on the porch wall. I showed it to Murphy, but he didn't seem impressed.

Men being boys. It's wonderful. We all share the philosophy that you should start slow and taper off. I can talk to these guys with free mind, like I did with Murphy, except they talk back. I don't think Murphy was jealous because he was much prettier than most of these dudes.

Life is not simple—unless you were Murphy. The world is a little crazy and it is hard to sift through all the crap sometimes—except at a Porch Hog meeting over hot coffee, with the banter of patrons and clucking of chickens in the background. It is a time to muddle through a variety of national pastimes: political scandals; suing each other; being insulted by stupid TV commercials; and, of course, sorting out how our Congress can spend so much of our money and get so little accomplished. These are serious topics, topics I couldn't run by Murphy because they require debate and solutions, and there is plenty of that at our meetings, though I'm not sure how practical our solutions are. Now that I think about it, I'm not sure how practical our elected official's solutions are.

Health is frequently a topic during Porch Hog meetings. Being retired also means you are older. The Porch Hogs figured out we have probably used about seventy-five percent of our life; that's just the way it is. But, we all figure there's no harm in taking action to extend longevity and quality of living. To that end, we each share new information, such as: eat things with antioxidants; drink green tea; flaxseed oil may help this and that; and of course the fish oil pill. The fish oil pill, even encapsulated, has a terrible odor and, here's a warning for you—don't bite into it. I was curious, so I did. That is the foulest tasting and smelling stuff in the universe. I gagged, made noises, tried to wash it out. Murphy was watching me like I was crazy, so I blew into his face so he could share my dilemma. He gagged, sneezed, left the room and refused to get on the couch with me later. I should have put a pill in his mouth.

If you research a lot of the stuff that is alleged to cure or prevent ailments, you find that you need to drink twenty gallons a day or eat a truckload a week to get the benefit. Nothing's simple.

I gave Murphy all kinds of stuff—some natural, some manmade. I wanted him to feel good and hang around a while, so he got a variety of supplemental health pills. He didn't mind. He'd eat anything I gave him; in and down like a vacuum cleaner. Except for carrots.

Carrots are great for dogs, especially those little baby carrots. Cleans their teeth, helps their gums, aids in digestion. It's the only food in the world Murphy would not eat. My son's dogs eats 'em like candy—begs for 'em. When I put one in Murphy dogs mouth, he would spit it out—not drop it—spit it out. It was very becoming. I mentioned this at a Porch Hog meeting and one member said I should just put something on it, like gravy, or wrap it in bread. Result: he rolled it around in his mouth until the gravy was gone, then spit out the carrot. As for the bread trick; have you ever seen a dog chew up a half slice of bread and swallow it while not damaging the carrot also in his mouth, which of course he then spat out. It isn't easy. I tried it. Another Porch hog solution that fell short of successful.

Every man, and woman, needs a special gang of their own gender where things can be said and heard with the confidence that 'what's said there stays there.' Free speak. I never worried that Murphy would spread rumors after hearing some of my ranting. Likewise, I feel comfortable with Porch Hog free speak. It's a code. To violate it would be unthinkable. Jokes are an exception. Those suitable for re-telling are subsequently shared outside the group. It is amazing how many really funny politician jokes there are—wonder if there is a reason for that. When I heard one I wanted to share with other's, I would practice on Murphy. There's an art to telling a good joke, you know. He never got it. At least his yawn suggested he didn't.

The Porch Hogs heard many Murphy stories. They always asked about him when I showed up, though only two had ever seen him. Some encouraged me to bring him one morning. I wish I had. He would have fit right in. There would have been jokes about his ears, or that famous nub, and he would have loved it.

I should have taken him. I could have driven the car instead of the cycle—no big deal. He was there in spirit as I would regale the gang with his latest antics, but I should have taken him. It's terrible when you think of things you should have done when it's too late.

Particularly bad when you should have done something and could have done it with a minor investment of time or energy.

Trust, two timing, experiments

I make the eighty mile trip to Alachua, Florida, to visit my folks every few days. Murphy accompanied me on those trips frequently, watching the scenery go by with his head hanging out the window. It must have been frightening to those we passed, seeing large wind blown jowls and flapping ears. I'm sure the ears made some sound as we passed, perhaps like a parachute canopy opening.

At some point on those trips, I could trust the fact that one of Murphy dog's very long, very thick slobber strings would be wrapped around the back of my head. The string was an end result of monstrous jaws acting as an air tunnel as we sped along. It was part of a routine precipitated by Murphy's desire to stop for a break. He let me know this by placing his head over the backseat, adjacent to my right ear, and barking. The slobber string was propelled around me with the force of his request. I could always trust him to do this. It was intentional because with my bath, I would also need to stop for a break. I toweled slobber from my head and neck while he marked new territory.

Trust comes in many forms. This variety falls under the predictable behavior category—I could trust that it was going to happen. I trusted Murphy to do his break alert and he delivered, with amenities.

When walking in the wilderness area we enjoyed, I daydreamed, paying no attention to what was ahead. I was comfortable doing that because if a snake was in the path, Murphy would let me know. I trusted him to do that and he did, more than once. Another form of trust.

Trust should be mutual and with Murphy it always was. One cannot always assume that with people. Recently, I took my car to a shop for a tire rotation. I parked in the service lane, and as I stepped out I noticed a blue chalk mark on the driver side front tire. Since I had left the downtown area just moments before, I deducted that it was a parking zone enforcement timing mark. I've seen these marks several times, and on more than one occasion, the mark was accompanied by a parking ticket—proof that some bureaucratic systems work. Anyway, the service guy drove the car into a bay, and I sought out the free coffee. Now, the deal here is I trusted those guys to rotate my tires, and they trusted me to pay them when they did that. Mutual trust. In this case however, I paid my bill, walked to the car and guess what was on the driver side front tire. They didn't rotate the tires. The situation was resolved after a bunch of defensive, stuttering explanations, but I haven't been back. Murphy would not have understood that breech of trust.

When I left Murphy alone in the house, he would not relieve himself because he trusted me to return and save him in the nick of time and he knew I trusted him to do his part. If, however, I left an open bag of chips on the table, I knew I could trust him to drag the bag down and consume the contents. He didn't destroy any trust by doing that because he knew I knew he'd do it, so it was on me.

I could even trust my behavior to Murphy. When I decided to act like an idiot, Murphy would not only condone this action, he would act like an idiot as well.

I hated it when Murphy dog trusted me to do something and I didn't. Oh, the look. Like when I had to stop taking him to the Q with me. The Q is a small place, fenced, just down the road where friends stay. It was our habit, Murphy and I, to stroll down to the Q each morning after his initial yard marking. I sipped coffee while Murphy checked out the other yard. It was something he looked forward to. Then Noodles arrived. My son's cat. Another inheritance. Anyway, our cat Cheddar was still alive and they were both males, so not a good idea to loose Noodles on Cheddar's property. Solution, the Q. Screened back porch, nice yard, perfect cat bachelor pad, with the door propped open to allow entry.

Noodles had never been around dogs, so I still went to the Q every morning to feed the beast, but Murphy had to stay behind; staring through the driveway gate as I disappeared down the street. It was terrible. I know he thought he was being punished because his look told me he didn't understand the situation. To make matters worse, after a few days of this intolerable situation, Murphy and I were taking a late afternoon walk to the boat ramp, and as we passed the Q, Noodles, now very much at home, strolled across the yard, stopped at the gate, and meowed. Murphy looked from the cat to me; about three times. His look was one of hurt, betrayal, of—you two-timing ass! It was terrible. It was as if he yelled at me, "So this is why you started leaving me back."

Murphy dog's hurt was short lived. He still trusted me. That's the way he was; the way most dogs are. Someone once offered an experiment you could try to both witness the depth of your dogs trust and compare that to people: put your dog and your wife in a car trunk for one hour, then open it and see who is happier to see you and who forgives you faster.

Our dogs trust us completely, without conditions. Studies have shown that people with pets, particularly dogs, seem happier and in many cases, live longer. I believe a large part of that is because we know that and it makes us feel good. To be trusted so completely.

Some things are important; others—not so much

I should take Murphy's water bowl out. Maybe tomorrow.

Old habits are hard to break. I don't need to keep leaving the light on for the old beast with diminished eye sight, or ensure the bedroom door is shut so he won't climb on the bed then fall off on his ass. There's no need to move stuff off the couch to make room for him. The office trash can he was so fond of knocking over can be left out of the closet, and I don't have to hurry home to let him out. I'll eventually quit doing all those things.

I can't move the path, though. The one that's about a foot wide and six inches deep leading from the front yard to the back. Murphy's path, made by countless trips with those huge feet. It will eventually fill in; probably faster if I quit walking in it. I need to do that. Right now though, I think I'll go back up to the man room... in the path.

Murphy has been gone one week today.

I started writing this the day after he died in one of those small four by six inch leather bound memo books. No particular reason for that choice. It was there. Besides, the nice leather cover is a shade of brown very much like the Murphy dog's color.

Writing has always been an outlet for me. I have written some mediocre books that a few folks have read, but sometimes I write just for myself. I think better doing that. I solve things. I have revelations. Everyone should write. That's what I tell students and book clubs. It's good for the soul, like having a one way discussion where you can dictate the subject, pace, characters, and outcome. It puts you in control.

Murphy's passing was very hard to handle. I cried a lot, 'like a little girl', as one of my friends would say. I never cried much, but I cried a lot the last few days. At some point down range, I'll read this. When I do, I think I may find out some things about myself. Murphy had that effect on me. He caused me to rethink things, to relax, to realize some things are important, some things, maybe most things, not so much. Fifteen years is a long time. A lot of stuff happens in fifteen years. I would have changed without Murphy, but I'm not sure it would have been in the same way. I sacrificed for Murphy the past several months. No, it wasn't a sacrifice; I helped him. He needed help so I helped him. I wanted to. It didn't bother me. Our connection went way beyond master and pet, man and dog. I don't totally understand it, but I do understand how deeply he affected me. I have grieved over dogs before. Tiffer was a great dog and I missed her terribly. I don't think I loved Murphy more, but he became a part of me. I shared things with him that no other living thing will ever know. I made him something that he probably was not, but that's okay when it occurs naturally, without effort. Were I to share these thoughts with other people, there are some out there who would understand. They would cry; then they would smile. But they would understand.

I'm on the last page of this cute little memo book, with its Murphy color cover. Though a piece of me died with him, I'm smiling as I recall the dog who brought laughter into the household; unpretentious, by just being... My self-imposed task, was to fill this book with the Murphy dog. I've done that, and I hope he approves. Somehow, I think he will.

About the Author

Randy Cribbs, shown here with Murphy is a native of Florida. A retired Army officer, he is the recipient of a 2009 Moonbeam Young Adult Horror/Mystery Silver Medal; a 2009 FWA Royal Palm Literary Best Book Award; 2009 Eric Hoffer Book Award Finalist; two 2007 FPA President's Best Book Awards; a 2006 FWA Royal Palm Literary Best Book Award and was selected as a Much Ado About Books featured author. He holds degrees from the University of Florida, Pacific Lutheran University, Jacksonville State University, and is a graduate of the FBI National Academy and the Armed Forces Staff College. He is the author of seven books: 'Were You There?, Vietnam Notes'; 'Tales From the Oldest City'; 'One Summer In The Old Town'; 'Illumination Rounds' ; 'The Vessel..tinaja: an Ancient City Mystery' ; 'Ancient City Treasures' ; and 'Ghosts: Another Summer in the Old Town'. He currently resides in St. Augustine, Florida. www.bn.com ; www.amazon.com; www.somestillserve.com

www.ingramcontent.com/pod-product-compliance
Lightning Source LLC
Chambersburg PA
CBHW051449290426
44109CB00016B/1680